Censorship in the Third Reich
A Case Study on John Dos Passos

AF280822

Miguel Araújo Oliveira was born in Hamburg, Germany, and has lived in Portugal for nearly three decades. He teaches at several universities in Lisbon. He is the author of monographs on the writers John Dos Passos, Günter Grass, and Ödön von Horváth. In addition to his academic work, Oliveira has published several works of fiction, poetry, and drama, such as *Salazar's Angels of Death*, which was published as part of the fiftieth anniversary of the Carnation Revolution in 2024.

Miguel Araújo Oliveira

Censorship in the Third Reich
A Case Study on John Dos Passos

Bibliographic information of the German National Library
The German National Library lists this publication in the
German National Bibliography; detailed bibliographic
data is available on the Internet at dnb.dnb.de.

© 2025, Miguel Araújo Oliveira
Publisher: BoD · Books on Demand GmbH,
In de Tarpen 42, 22848 Norderstedt
Print: Libri Plureos GmbH, Friedensallee 273,
22763 Hamburg
ISBN: 978-3-7693-2787-8

for my nieces
Nicole and Melanie

Contents

Acknowledgements

Words cannot express my gratitude to my family, mother, sister, brother-in-law, and nieces for their love, support, and constant encouragement.

I am also deeply indebted to Charles Townsend Ludington for his insight and unfading interest in my work. Towny, as he always signed his correspondence with me, sadly passed away in 2021. He will be greatly missed.

I would like to express my appreciation to Rosa Bautista, too, for having shared with me her knowledge and significant material on the Spanish censorship reports on John Dos Passos.

In addition, I am very obliged to Jessica Teague for having alerted me to an important letter she found archived at the Special Collections Library of the

University of Virginia in the "Dos Passos Papers" pertaining to censorship that she kindly shared with me.

Moreover, I am grateful to Isgard Löffler at the *Bundesarchiv, Abteilung DDR* (Federal Archive, section German Democratic Republic) for corresponding with me about the *Druckgenehmigungen* (printing permissions) on Dos Passos, which I was allowed to quote in this work.

Furthermore, I am thankful to Thomas Überfoff, the editorial director at Rowohlt, for his correspondence about the reedition of German translations of Dos Passos's novels in the postwar era.

Besides, I can't express enough my sincere gratitude to Irakli Tskhvediani, Professor at the Akaki Tsereteli State University, who kindly invited me to present my studies on Dos Passos and censorship at his prestigious college in Georgia, even though, unfortunately, the weather conspired against us so that my flight was delayed, and I was unable to attend the international conference that was nevertheless a great success.

Finally, I would like to extend my acknowledgement to the Dos Passos's family, in particular to Lucy Hamlin Dos Passos Coggin, and to John Dos Passos Coggin, who have always been genuinely interested and helpful in more ways than one.

Introduction

In this monograph, I will explain why John Dos Passos's books were burned and later on forbidden during the Third Reich. The Nazis accused Dos Passos's writings of being modernist, immoral, anti-militarist, and either anarchist or communist and therefore added Dos Passos's name to the "*Schwarze Liste*,"[1] the Nazis' infamous 'black list' of unwanted writers and banned book titles.

The circumstances of other authors, whose works had also been prohibited, such as Erich Kästner and Oskar Maria Graf, will be referred to, as well, as to better illustrate the dimension of censorship and the real damage caused to canonical literature in the Third Reich, while referring, of course, to Paul

---

[1] All translations in this monograph are the author's own, unless otherwise noted.

Baudisch, Julian Gumperz, and Klaus Lambrecht too, John Dos Passos's German translators, who had to flee the country because of their own political consciousness.

Whereas the Nazis prohibited all *Asphaltliteratur* ("asphalt literature"), like John Dos Passos's novel *Manhattan Transfer*, they now sought after a new form of writing that they named: *Blut und Boden Literatur* (blood and soil literature), *Heimatliteratur* (homeland literature), and *Weihedichtung* (literature of consecration), on which this book also provides some brief comments, to contrast and clarify why John Dos Passos did not fit into these categories.

Moreover, I will focus on what time in the post-war era John Dos Passos was republished in East and West Germany.

Officially no censorship existed in the German Democratic Republic, yet the truth is that editors eventually had to ask for printing permission. I shall refer to and comment on the so far unnoted printing permits concerning John Dos Passos's novels and explain how they interrelate with censorship.

Contextualization

"Das war der Anfang nur, dort wo man Bücher verbrennt, verbrennt man am Ende gar Menschen."

"This was only the beginning; wherever you burn books, you also burn people in the end."

Heinrich Heine

The epigraph above might be one of the most cited to introduce monographs and articles on censorship. Its author, the German writer Heinrich Heine (1797-1856), had been a victim of censorship himself. During his lifetime, his works had been, at first, prohibited in the kingdom of Prussia and, later on, in almost all of the German small states. His writings were considered blasphemous and obscene.

Yet there was another reason for his prohibition. In his writings, Heine attacked institutions of the reign, as well as the Prussian king Friedrich Wilhelm III, whom Heine accused of having promised to his people a constitution, but to have purposefully failed to implement such a constitutional monarchy in his kingdom throughout his lifetime. Heine's works were thus severely censored and their circulation outlawed in Prussia.

Fearing for his own safety, Heine moved to Paris in 1832. Sometime earlier, in the 1820's, Heine had published his play *Almansor*, in which he commented on censorship and the suppression of 'heresy' by the church. He put the famous words, "this was only the beginning, wherever you burn books, you also burn people in the end" (2006: 137), in the mouth of a Moslem, who herewith acts in response to the burning of the holy Quran by a Catholic Cardinal in Granada.

Today one might claim that Heine's cautioning against the intertwining of censorship and murder became reality, not only under the Spanish Inquisition, but as well under Adolf Hitler.

Within this context, *Censorship in the Third Reich* essentially aims at explaining why the books by the American writer of Portuguese ancestry, John Dos Passos, had been burned and banned in Hitler's Germany.

In point of fact, the famous writer had been censored in many countries of different political regimes, which feared the power that Dos Passos's influencing novels could have upon its readership.

Even though the majority of people nowadays think that censorship only occurs in dictatorships, the truth is, as denoted by Konrad Becker in *Die Politik der Infosphäre* (*The Politics of the Infosphere*), that

> No society—neither in the past nor in the present—is entirely without censorship. Not only authoritarian regimes, but also democratic societies are not free from attempts to prevent the publication and dissemination of certain information. (2002: 87)

Even John Dos Passos's writings, as we will see hereinafter, had been forbidden in several dictatorships and monarchies as well as in democratic countries, where, contrary to the widespread belief in the prevalence of non-censorship, freedom of speech may also be restricted.

Nineteen Nineteen, for instance, had been banned in 1932 as "indecent and obscene" in Australia ("Australian Book Censorship" 1935: 10), but also in Ireland, where the Publications Act, ratified in 1929, prohibited for the same reasons John Dos Passos's *Manhattan Transfer*, *The 42nd Parallel*, and *Nineteen Nineteen*. (See

Cooney 2000: 242) Even though Dos Passos's novels were published under Stalin in the Soviet Union, they only appeared "in abridged form." (Sherry 2015: 67)

Moreover, Dos Passos had been forbidden in his own country. Having contacted through e-mail correspondence Charles Townsend Ludington, the authority and authorized biographer of John Dos Passos, I was made aware that Dos Passos's trilogy *U.S.A.* had been "banned from public schools in Texas in the 1940's," even though "that did not last very long."

Yet, also in Boston, Massachusetts, several pressure groups like the "Clean Books League," the "Women's Christian Temperance Union," and the "Watch and Ward Society" barred Dos Passos's *Manhattan Transfer* from public libraries. (Petersen 1995: 293)

So-called "bookleggers" sold the indexed novels on the black market since the majority of bookshops got rid of the blacklisted titles. Those that did not were boycotted and menaced with bankruptcy. (Boyer 2002: 177)

Another severe pressure group was the "National Organization for Decent Literature" (known as NODL), which "was officially sponsored and supervised by the US Catholic bishops." (Jones 2015: 1683) According to NODL's "code," they, too, recommended Dos Passos's *The 42nd Parallel* for prohibition (Lockhardt 1954: 318) for using "blasphemous, profane [and] obscene speech." (Jones 2015: 1684)

Furthermore, *Manhattan Transfer* had been generally banned "from the U.S. mails under the Comstock Act," a "federal bill," which proscribed "every obscene, lewd, lascivious or filthy book [...] of an indecent character" to circulate through the countries' post offices. (Green 2005: 122-123)

Even though these foolish accusations cry out for a rectifying commentary, they have to be left out of the scope of this work.

As stated afore, my work will limit itself to the barring of Dos Passos in the Third Reich, even though I might briefly refer further ahead to Dos Passos's suffering of censorship in Italy, Poland, Portugal, and Spain, but only to better distinguish censorship practices with those in force in Nazi Germany.

My study supports the more recent views by scholars on the 1933 book burnings, which claim that the *Bücherverbrennung* (*auto-de-fé*) was organized by university students to curry favor with the *Führer* and thus to maintain and expand their power at the universities.

With the same end in view, the scholar Hans-Wolfgang Strätz had access to the students' league correspondence, which evidences the fact that the idea of burning books was brought up by the students and not, as it has been claimed in the past, by Nazi government officials, and that it was the students who were behind the entire organization, not the censorship office, which, as a matter of fact, was only created some months after the book burning took place.

Expressing this conviction is in no way to be interpreted as revisionist, aiming at excusing or whitewashing in any form the Nazi terror, but it strives for explaining that Hitler's dictatorship depended from its very beginning on the collaboration and the further reaching voluntary self-initiative of the German people (in this case the upcoming generation of intellectuals), who created synergies for the Nazi movement.

Eventually, the Nazi regime thanked the students' league, granting it favors and giving the students the arbitral power to select unpopular professors that they charged with being Un-German, so that these could be fired from their teaching positions or be sent to the concentration camps, where they eventually found death.

Censorship in the Third Reich

With the so-called *Machtergreifung* (Hitler's rise to power), intellectuals, among them a few librarians, professors of German Studies, and, in particular, students—all of them adherent to the Nazi *Weltanschauung* (worldview)—called out for censorship. They were against liberty and freedom since they had been educated according to the maxim "*Gehorsam und Pflichterfüllung*," which meant to be obedient and to honor their duty fulfillment towards their fatherland. (Schmidt 2008: 21)

These beliefs were propagandized in school, where pupils were expected to learn materials by rote, repeating them until they could recite them by heart.

The education system aimed not at making the subject matter comprehensible. Questioning, reflecting, discussing, understanding, and expressing one's opinion were therefore totally objected to.

The teacher's point of view was never to be questioned. He was always right, and he could punish his students even physically (*Züchtigung*), whenever they were not submissive and respectful. A good Wilhelmenian teacher had to be authoritarian, strict, and severe.

When the Weimar Republic replaced the monarchy, the republicans were unable to substitute the old guard of monarchists who had been occupying positions of importance in the German schools, universities, and the entire administration, including the judicial apparatus.

Since professors were not dismissed in the newly proclaimed Republic but maintained their teaching positions, it comes as no surprise that their way of educating their students remained the same, which essentially inhibited free thinking as well as the ability to analyze and question old creeds and convictions and to dare the liberty to oppose them.

This disapproving and repressing approach, of course, was by no means democratic in its pedagogy. Ultimately, this meant that the Weimar Republic was from its very beginning "a republic without republicans." The German writer Heinrich Mann was well aware of this fact and lamented:

> Justice was never republican; everyone saw that: the *Reichswehr* [the military organization responsible for the defense of Germany] was not, nor were the universities. No part of the administration was. (Schröter 2002: 117)

Hoping the German people could be brought to reason and led to embrace and cherish freedom, the writers Kurt Tucholsky and Carl von Ossietzky expressed in their weekly magazine *Die Weltbühne* (*The World Stage*) "sharp criticism towards the survival of Wilhelminian ideas of order in the German bureaucracy." (Balzer 1990: 389)

Unfortunately, influencing the German people to esteem liberty proved unmanageable during this era. The Great Depression of 1929 had meant not only the loss of employment but also the loss of faith in the democratic government and the presidency of Friedrich Ebert. People asked what good freedom was if they couldn't make a living from it.

The implementation of freedom and democracy in the Weimar Republic was therefore difficult, permanently boycotted, and even sabotaged. Democracy was demonized since the traditionalists did not believe the German people capable of self-governance, and they regarded the Republic as a dangerous experiment. They feared that liberty would bring chaos and immorality.

Ossietzky, who demanded a revolution instead of a reformation of the people's political involvement, understanding, and schooling, was more than once fined. He was eventually sentenced to prison for his audacity in 1931.

Two years later, now under the Nazis, *Die Weltbühne* was suppressed, and Ossietzky was once more arrested, while Tucholsky fled the country.

Yet, as noted above, already during the first German republic, attempts were made to silence opponents; fining and arresting them were just two of a numerous strategies to get rid of them.

Actually, the Weimar constitution of 1919 "guaranteed German citizens the right 'to express his opinion freely' [...] and announced that 'there is no censorship'"; the truth is, though, that this right was contradicted by a subparagraph that allowed "legal measures [... to be taken] in order to combat trashy and obscene literature." (Lewy 2016: 3)

However, democracy and freedom of speech were not only fought against by old monarchists in Weimar Germany.

Already in 1928, the Nazi Alfred Rosenberg headed the *Kampfbund für deutsche Kultur* (Fighting League for German Culture), which aimed to squash all forms of artistic expression that challenged the views of the NSDAP (*Nationalsozialistische Deutsche Arbeiterpartei*—the National-Socialist German Workers' Party) by accusing works of art of being pornographic and obscene.

Even though not yet in power, the Nazis succeeded in issuing a bill "against the culture of the Negroes and for German National Tradition." (Lewy 2016: 5) Herewith, they hoped to expurgate the jazz, which had become popular in the German nightclubs.

Furthermore, they blue-penciled books such as Erich Maria Remarque's *Im Westen nichts Neues* (*All Quiet on the Western Front*), an anti-war novel that had reached the status of a worldwide best-seller with 26 translations in its first year of publication.

Even the premiere of the film version in Berlin was barred in September 1930[2].

---

[2] The film had been produced by the German Jew Carl Laemmle, President of Universal Studios in the United States. Even though the film won two Academy Awards, it was considered by the Nazis a *Judenfilm* (Jewish film). The Nazis bought 200 tickets for the premiere at the Berlin *Mozartsaal* with the intent to blast the premiere by protesting aloud, causing a brawl, and releasing white mice

This shows clearly that also the Nazis had been successful in undermining freedom of expression in the Weimar Republic in cooperation with the courts of law, which were still chaired by judges of the *ancien régime.*

As discussed, teachers and professors of the bygone monarchist regime, among others, destabilized the fragile attempts to democratize Germany and to establish its republic. They were still indoctrinating blind obedience rather than instructing their students to make good use of freedom.

Obviously, and as expected, the majority of students embraced thus the totalitarian ideology that had been presented to them from their earliest

---

during the screening of the film so that panic was spread within the theatre. The exhibition of the film was thereupon forbidden.

school days as a safe alternative to the Weimar Republic.

In 1926, the NSDStB (*Nationalsozialistischer Deutscher Studentenbund* — National-Socialist German Students' League) was founded to support the Nazis. (Schneider 2013: 4) The members of the league believed that national-socialism would bring unemployment solutions and end the social-political crisis, which they believed the Weimar Republic was unable to solve. Hence many students, wearing Nazi uniforms and the swastika, voted for the NSDAP.

Now, after having won the elections on January 30, 1933, the Nazis were taking over the power and starting to overthrow the Republic. Many professors, librarians, and students hailed the end of democracy and felt it was now their time to act, too, by calling out for censorship and the end of freedom of speech, which they had been taught to perceive as a menace to their world.

In the midst of the euphoria of the Nazis' victory, a librarian in Berlin, Dr. Wolfgang Herrmann, started to produce *Schwarze Listen* (black lists), on which he registered writers whose works he wanted banned. Already in his first draft, John Dos Passos's name is recorded.

Herrmann sent these lists of "*schädliches und unerwünschtes Schrifttum*" (harmful and undesirable literature) to fellow librarians, students, and their principals. In his attached letters, he demanded to eliminate from the public libraries the blacklisted authors and their works.

Yet, in his ambition to become the country's *Inquisitor Generalis*, Wolfgang Herrmann also referred derogatively to Adolf Hitler's *Mein Kampf*, asserting that it contained no original and theoretically grounded ideas (see Ehm 2013: 5); furthermore, he had openly questioned Hitler's "mental acuity." (Lewy 2016: 16) That might have been sufficient reason for the Ministry of Propaganda to never officially approve of Herrmann's lists.

On their "own initiative" (Gussek 2009: 22), students of the DSt (*Deutsche Studentenschaft* — German Students' League) now came up with the idea of burning books to prove themselves to the newly elected Nazi authorities.

The DSt did not belong to the Nazi party and had therefore lost its power within the universities to the NSDStB. By planning the book burnings all by themselves, the students of the DSt tried to present themselves as trustworthy and reliable to promote Nazi politics at all university levels. Herewith they hoped it possible to claim back authority to represent the students' interests and knock the rivaling NSDStB off its pedestal. (Strätz 1968: 349-50)

The DSt prepared a "manifest" entitled "*Wider den undeutschen Geist*" (Against the Un-German spirit), in which the students enumerated 12 bullet points as the organization's goals, some of them reading:

> (3) The purity of language and literature depends on you!
> (4) Our most dangerous enemy is the Jew and those who are in bondage to him.
> (5) The Jew can only think in Jewish terms. If he writes in German, he lies. The German who writes in German but thinks in an Un-German way is a traitor!
> (6) We want to eradicate lies, we want to brand treason, we do not want our schools to be places of thoughtlessness, but of discipline and political education. [...] (7) We demand of censorship: Jewish works are published [from now on] in

Hebrew. If they appear in German, they are to be marked as translations. [We demand a harsh] intervention against the abuse of the German written language. The German written word is only available to the German people. The Un-German spirit must be eradicated from public libraries. (Schneider 2013: 5)

In stating this, the students required public and university libraries to be purged of unwanted writers, especially if they were *Volljuden* ("full-Jews") or of Jewish lineage (*Halbjuden* or *Mischlinge*),[3] conveying to the Nazis' policy of *Entjudung* (a Nazi jargon standing for '*de-Jewification*'). Hereby, the students stated to share with the Nazis their racist and anti-Semitic viewpoints.

Additionally, the students' league demanded of each fellow student to

---

[3] Pejorative terms used by the Nazis to refer to "half-Jews" or people of both Aryan and non-Aryan descent.

"cleanse his own library of everything that [was] Un-German" and to "inspect the library of his acquaintances," too, while the DSt itself was supposed to eliminate black-listed authors from public libraries. (Krischke 1998a: 224)

As "self-appointed judges of literature," these students now started to invade those libraries, removing from the shelves those books and authors they thought unfit for others to read. (Gussek 2009: 22.)

The books were herded onto trucks and into private cars, and they were stored at the DSt's head offices since the students had agreed to organize a *Sommerfest* (summer "festivity"), in which they would publically burn these books. (Gussek 2009: 23)

While plundering the public libraries, students made librarians sign a reassurance that stated:

> I hereby assure that I will remove the books on the blacklist [...] from my library [...]. I am aware that loaning these books will result in judicial penalties. (Strätz 1968: 364)

These penalties, however, were still extralegal and therefore not binding. Nonetheless, these intimidations, which in some cases included physical violence, were vigorous enough so that the majority of librarians conformed to the students' exigencies.

In the meantime, the students had further decided to create a "*Schandpfahl*" (post of shame).

> We will create a post of shame! We will place such a stake in front of all colleges. A chunky tree trunk [...]. At that stake, we will nail the products of those who are not of our mind. And we will leave that pale forever. As long as we need it.

> Today for writers, tomorrow for professors. (Krischke 1998a: 224-5)

The students of the DSt tore the covers of the book blocks and nailed them at the *Schandpfahl*, with the intention to publicly denounce these writers and their works.

Moreover, the *Schandpfahl* was supposed to alert people who passed by that the works nailed to it were considered shameful to possess or to read. The students hoped that the ordinary people would inspect their libraries at home and remove the undesired volumes.

The post of shame had yet another function. It served to intimidate and silence university professors that did not agree with National-Socialism, and who condemned the new *Weltanschauung* in their lectures and seminars. By exposing them publically on the *Schandpfahl* the students factually threatened not only their position as professors but also their lives.

Among the threatened was, for instance, the philosophy professor Johannes Maria Verweyen, who was dismissed from the University of Bonn in 1934 after a series of critical lectures on racial fanaticism. It was the students who had given away Verweyen to the university authorities. Right afterward, Verweyen's publications were blacklisted and he was arrested by the Gestapo—*Geheime Staatspolizei* (Secret State Police). He was murdered in 1945 in the concentration camp Bergen-Belsen.

Another professor who had been persecuted was Kurt Huber of the Maximilian University of Munich. His classes were regularly disrupted by Nazi students since, like Verweyen, he dared to criticize openly in his lectures Hitler's crimes. By means of intimidation, groups of students tried to forbid Huber to speak. In the end, he—who, in the meantime, had made friends with Hans and Sophie Scholl as well as with Alexander Schmorell, all members of the *Weiße Rose* (White Rose), a freethinking underground student resistance group[4]—was arrested and guillotined.

Professor Emil Julius Gumbel also lost his professorship at the University of Heidelberg. Already in 1921, he had written a monograph, *Zwei Jahre politischer Mord* (*Two years of political murder*), in which he criticized the Nazis, who wouldn't stop at murder on their way to power. Gumbel was also harassed by university students who banished his books. He lost his *Lehrbefugnis* (teaching credential) and

---

[4] Apart from Hans and Sophie Scholl and Alexander Schmorell, Christoph Probst and Willi Graf were also members.

decided to flee to New York, where he taught at the University of Columbia until his death in 1966.

Announcement posters by the theology professor Dietrich Bonhoeffer were regularly taken down by students at the Technical University of Berlin. By 1936, Bonhoeffer was banned from public speaking and publishing texts. In 1945, he too was murdered by hanging at the concentration camp Flossenbürg.

Theodor Litt, was intimidated by students in Leipzig and thus lost his professorial chair in 1937; Moritz Schlick was shot dead by Johann Nelböck, a student of his, at the University of Vienna. Even though sentenced to ten years of prison, Nelböck, who used his trial to disseminate his racist and anti-Semitic beliefs, became right after the Annexation of Austria somewhat of a hero among his fellow students and was released from the penitentiary; Ernst von Aster, President of the German League for Human Rights, was dismissed from his post as philosophy professor at the University of Gießen and sought for exile in Sweden; Jonas Cohn, Ernst Cassirer, Werner Gottfried Brock, Albert Einstein, the list would be too long if an attempt was to be made to write down all the names of professors who were expelled from university, killed, or had to flee the country or the annexed territories.

This brain drain would later prove disastrous for the Third Reich, even though its new intellectuals would never admit it due to their blind nationalism, stupid arrogance, and their erroneous belief in their Aryan superiority, which they tried to prove in supposedly "scientific" subjects like *Rassenkunde* (racial studies) and *Erbgesundheitslehre* (eugenics).

Martin Heidegger, who in May 1933 took over the position as rector *magnificus* of the University of Freiburg, claimed to have resisted to remove books by Jewish authors from the university library, referring, for instance, to the works of his professor, Edmund Husserl, whom Heidegger mentioned and quoted in his own academic work. (Cf. Heidegger 1976: 199)

He further claimed to have been pressured by a group of students to post an announcement at the university bulletin board that spread anti-Semitism. He allegedly refused, even when menaced by the S.A. (*Sturmabteilung*—Stormtroopers).

> On the second day I took office, the student leader appeared in the rector's office with two companions and once again demanded that the Jewish poster be put up. I refused. The three students left with the remark that the ban would be reported to the Reich's student leadership. After a few days, a [...] call

> [...] came from the top S.A.-*Führer*. [...]
> He demanded that the poster be
> displayed as it was already displayed at
> other universities. [...] Nevertheless, I did
> not withdraw my ban. (Heidegger 1976:
> 196)

All over again, it was the students who applied pressure. Heidegger found himself in an inextricable situation. According to his students, his ideological 'misconduct' had to be reported to the S.A.. This could have meant imprisonment or worse.

Yet nothing alike happened. The truth is that Heidegger had hailed Hitler's rise to *Reichskanzler* (chancellor of the Reich), believing that a strong man (a dictator) was needed to straighten out the country.[5] (Cf. Heidgger 1976: 196)

---

[5] Heidegger later claimed to have dissociated from National Socialism by 1934, the year he resigned from office as rector. Yet it may be questioned if he

Endorsing the Nazi regime, Heidegger's inauguration speech as rector at the University of Freiburg was fairly validating the efforts by the Nazis. When addressing the students in his infamous speech "The Self-Assertion of the German University," he stated:

> Out of the resoluteness of the German students to stand their ground while German destiny is in its most extreme distress comes a will to the essence of the university. [...] The much-lauded "academic freedom" will be expelled from the German university; for this

really detached himself from the Nazi *Weltanschauung*. In his *Schwarze Hefte* (black notebooks), written between 1931 and 1975, Heidegger explicitly questioned if the Jews were really the victims and if the responsibility of World War II was not to be attributed to the Jews rather than to the German people. In his letters to his brother Fritz, Heidegger further revealed his admiration for the *Führer*. Heidegger even sent his brother a copy of Hitler's *Mein Kampf* as a Christmas gift.

freedom was not genuine because it was only negative. It primarily meant lack of concern, arbitrariness of intentions and inclinations, lack of restraint in what was done and left undone. The concept of the freedom of the German student is now brought back to its truth. (Qtd. in Neske 1990: 4)

Heidegger's concept of 'academic freedom' entailed a polemic and disreputable notion of self-determination. Actually, it consisted of its very opposite. What Heidegger and his students understood as freedom was more accurately subjugation based on censorship, the suppression, and the gagging of the truth, as well as the fabrication of 'scientific' lies that would serve the abominable and heinous causes of the Third Reich through the policy of *Gleichschaltung* (the enforced standardization of state institutions), like the universities and their purging of any opponents.

With the above mentioned, I want to reemphasize that the new *intelligentsia* not only proved to be a small but a very effective cog in Hitler's totalitarian machinery. The majority of students did not limit themselves, as shown, to following orders. They were eager to partake pro-actively by assuming control and initiative by means of denunciation, persecution of dissenting professors, and by prohibiting them to speak their minds, to write, and from being read.

In their endeavors, they were backed by some university professors who embraced (even if only temporarily or not) the devil's cause.[6]

---

[6] Among the Nazi-sympathizing scholars were Herman Grapow, Karl Haushofer, Emanuel Hirsch, Friedrich Neumann, Georg Wilhelm Pinder, etc..

By May 10, 1933, the aforementioned students of the DSt had stockpiled enough books to hold that solemn event with which they wanted to stress and celebrate the end of liberty and freedom in the country.

Even though the main festivity was to take place at the *Berliner Opernplatz* (Berlin's opera square), some other seventy German cities organized the *Bücherverbrennung* (book burning), too. In Bonn, Bremen, Dresden, Göttingen, and Kiel, among others, the *auto-de-fé* took place simultaneously on May 10, while in Hamburg it was on the 15, in Essen on June 21, and in Jena on August 26. In Mannheim, where the book burning occurred on May 19, the students not only burned books, but also the tricolor (*schwarz-rot-gold*—black-red-gold) flag of the Weimar Republic. (Strätz 1968: 368)

Scholars have long claimed that in Freiburg the book burning did not take place. The reason for this was an interview given by Martin Heidegger in September 1966 to the journalist Rudolf Augstein in *Der Spiegel*, where Heidegger alleged to have forbidden the *Bücherverbrennung* at his university. (Cf. Heidegger 1976: 198) The truth, however, was that the book burning did not take place in Freiburg as scheduled on June 17 because it was heavily raining. The book burning was postponed and occurred at the solstice that the Nazis celebrated on June 24, 1933. During the festivity at the university stadium, Heidegger even gave a speech in which he theatrically addressed his students by reassuring them, once more, of being one of them.

> "Fire! Tell us: You must not become blind in battle, but you must remain

bright for action. Flame! Your blaze proclaims to us: The German revolution does not sleep; it ignites anew and illuminates the path on which there is no turning back. [...] Flames ignite! Hearts burn!" (Heidegger, 2000: 131)

Contrary to what Heidegger claimed in the nineteen-sixties, it seems that he sanctioned the book burning; adding fuel to the fire with his appalling rhetoric.

The main *fête* in Berlin that counted on a large participation of the population—for students the participation was, of course, obligatory—included a *Fakelzug* (torchlight procession) and a pyre where at that night some estimated 20,000 books were burned and a plaster bust of the Jewish professor Magnus Hirschfeld,[7] one

---

[7] Hirschfeld, who had founded the Research Institute for Sexual Science in Berlin, had been physically attacked in the 1920's by Nazi supporters for being both homosexual and Jewish. In 1933, the institute's library was vandalized and completely

of the first outspoken advocates for homosexuality in Germany, was crushed. What remained of its head was impaled on a pole and swayed back and forth for the attending masses to see.

The students had prepared nine *Feuersprüche* (declarations to the fire), which they voiced pathetically before throwing the books into the flames. "Each declaration uses one or two headwords to denote the views and offenses that are contrary to the [new] German spirit." (Strätz 1968: 360) One of them went: "Against decadence and moral decay! [...] I hand over to the flames the writings by Heinrich Mann, Ernst Glaeser, and Erich Kästner." (Schneider 2013: 16)

Kästner claimed to have been present in Berlin, among thousands of people who

---

destroyed during the book burning. Of course, monographs authored by Hirschfeld were forbidden and burned, too. Magnus Hirschfeld fled to France, where he died only two years later, in 1935.

had come to attend the spectacle. Years later, Erich Kästner remarked to have felt appalled and aghast.

> And in 1933 my books were burned in Berlin, on the large square next to the State Opera, by a certain *Herr* Goebbels, with somber solemn pomp. He shouted in triumph the names of twenty-four German writers, who were to be wiped off symbolically forever. I was the only one of the twenty-four who had come in person to witness this theatrical impudence. I stood in front of the university, wedged between students in SA uniform, the blooms of the nation, I saw our books fly into the flickering flames and heard the lewd tirades of the little fake liar. [...] It was disgusting. (1997: 9)

Kästner also found the critics repulsive, who previously had greeted his works and now, after his prohibition, penned against him. He accused them of having a "selectable consciousness." (Enderle 1999: 66)

Contrary to many of his contemporaries, Erich Kästner did not go into exile when the Nazis rose to power. He had chosen the "*innere Migration*" ('internal exile' or 'inner emigration'), a term that essentially meant that these writers (among them Werner Bergengruen and Wolfgang Koeppen) did not turn their backs on their country and tried to continue publishing in Nazi Germany, writing between the lines, often enough running great risks for their lives. The same way Erich Kästner was many times harassed, even his bank account had been suspended by the authorities. Eventually, he was forbidden to publish and thus was deprived of any form of income for his upkeep. Several times he had been brought to the headquarters of the Gestapo, where he had passed hours for interrogation.

Among the authors that were burned that night in Berlin were John Dos Passos, Ernest Hemingway, Upton Sinclair, Jack London, James Joyce, Heinrich Heine, Lion Feuchtwanger, Vicki Baum, Alfred Döblin, Franz Kafka, Arthur Schnitzler, Franz Werfel, Frank Wedekind, Max Brod, Joachim Ringelnatz, Heinrich Mann, Stefan Zweig, and Sigmund Freud.

Freud was one of fifteen writers[8] that were mentioned by name before his books were tossed into the bonfires. The chant went:

> Against the soul-destroying overestimation of the sex life—and on behalf of the nobility of the human soul—I offer to the flames the writings of

---

[8] The other writers were Karl Marx, Karl Kautsky, Heinrich Mann, Ernst Glaeser, Erich Kästner, Friedrich Wilhelm Förster, Emil Ludwig, Werner Hegemann, Theodor Wolff, Georg Bernhard, Erich Maria Remarque, Alfred Kerr, Kurt Tucholsky, and Carl von Ossietzky.

one Sigmund Freud! (Blanchfield 2022:
n.p.)

Actually, Freud commented with great sarcasm on being burned: "What for progress! In the Medieval Ages they would have burned me; today they content themselves with burning my books." (Lohmann 2002: 91)

While the majority of authors were reacting with rage for being burned and banned, Oskar Maria Graf went mad because he was not blacklisted (with the exception of his masterpiece *Wir sind Gefangene—We are prisoners*). His protest, *Verbrennt mich* (burn me), read:

> I am called to be one of the exponents of the 'new' German spirit! In vain, I ask myself, how did I deserve this disgrace? The Third Reich has expelled almost all German works of importance; it has renounced the real German literature; it has hunted a large number of its

important writers into exile and made the appearance of their works impossible in Germany. [...] And the representatives of this barbarous nationalism that has nothing, absolutely nothing at all to do with being German are claiming that I am one of them; they have put me on their so-called 'white list,' which can only be a black list before the world conscience! I do not deserve this dishonor! After all my life and after all my writing, I have the right to demand that my books be given over to the pure flame of the pyre and not into the bloody hands and corrupted heads of a brown gang of murderers. (Schneider 2013: 24)

Shortly after his protest was printed, Oskar Maria Graf was declared by the Nazis *persona non grata*. Of course, Graf left Germany and never returned. He immigrated to the United States, where he obtained American citizenship, dying in New York in 1967.

In the past, many scholars (and even Erich Kästner in his testimony quoted above) attributed the organization of the book burning to the authorship of Dr. Joseph Goebbels, the *Reichsminister für Volksaufklärung und Propaganda* (Minister of Public Enlightenment and Propaganda), who in fact was present during the book burning.

However, current research shows that the German students, particularly members of the DSt, "independently planned [...] and staged" the book burning themselves. It is claimed that Joseph Goebbels was all but pleased regarding the free engagement of the students' league (see Brunner 2013: 18), since in his idealized dictatorship the ordinary people were supposed to wait for and follow orders and not to act autonomously without being asked.

Moreover, it is stated that Goebbels may "have foreseen that this *auto-de-fé* of books would do great damage to Germany's reputation abroad." (Lewy 2016: 10) Principally this is true, since overseas "the impact was immediate and forceful." In America, for instance, "editorial opinion was nearly unanimous in condemning this attack on intellectual freedom." (Lewy 2016: 14)

In the Third Reich, however, the press was not fawning enough, except for Rudolf Geck, "an editor of the reputable *Frankfurter Zeitung*" (*Frankfurter Newspaper*). In his article on the *Bücherverbrennung* he wrote: "It is an error, young gentlemen, to believe that the spirit of poets and thinkers can be defeated by the burning of books." (Lewy 2016: 14)

When invited by the president of the DSt to give a speech during the book burning ceremony, at midnight, Goebbels hesitatingly accepted. Yet, after realizing that some estimated 70,000 people had shown up, he gladly acknowledged in his diary entry that he did so.

In his *Brandrede* (also referred to as *Feuerrede*—fire speech), which Goebbels entitled: "*Der Geist ist erwacht*" (the [German] spirit is awakened), the Minister of Propaganda addressed the students, adverting:

> If you students have assumed the right to throw the mental filth into the flames, then you must also take the obligation to replace this garbage; (Girod 2012: 176)

Goebbels implied, of course, that the students should replace the critical works against Nazism with writings treating positively the new National-Socialist *Weltanschauung*.

The writer Ernst Toller, who at the time was already living in Switzerland, reacted in an open letter to Goebbels, stating:

You pretend to awaken the German youth, and yet you blind their minds, their eyes, and their voices. You pretend to save the German children, and yet you poison their hearts with the shameful phrases of stupid nationalism and racial hatred. (Krischke 1998a: 229)

Of course, the Nazis thought otherwise. The new authorities, in each of the German cities where the book burning took place, had supported the DSt in their demands for censorship. Among them mayors, the police force and fire departments had authorized the book burnings.

Yet, as stated before, at the time of the *Bücherverbrennung*, the ministerial apparatus that would regulate censorship in the Third Reich had not yet been officially created. As a matter of fact, Joseph Goebbels only inaugurated his *Reichskulturkammer* (Reich Chamber of

Culture) some months later, on September 22. The Reich Chamber of Culture had several sub-chambers for the arts (*Reichskammer der bildenden Künste*), literature (*Reichsschrifttumskammer*), theatre (*Reichstheaterkammer*), music (*Reichsmusikkammer*), film (*Reichsfilmkammer*), radio (*Reichsrundfunkkammer*) and the press (*Reichspressekammer*).

Only Aryans could be members of the chamber of literature. They were asked to certify for their pure German ancestry. To publish books in the Third Reich, the author had to be admitted as a member of the chamber otherwise, he would have been fined. Of course, this in itself was a censorial selection of who was to be authorized and whose works were inhibited from being dispersed throughout the Reich.

Even now, public libraries were unceasingly expurgated of Un-German writers. Henceforth, though, it was no longer the students who went into the libraries, but only the S.A. or the Gestapo.

Although a legal provision now existed to outlaw unwanted books, things did not work impeccably yet. Rivalry existed between the S.A., headed by Ernst Röhm, and the Gestapo, commanded by Hermann Göring. Many times the police did not even know what type of literature to seize. Furthermore, "certain books were forbidden in one state but not in others." (Lewy 2016: 23) It was only in 1936 that "book bans were [...] centralized" and thus countrywide forbidden. (Lewy 2016: 26)

John Dos Passos
burned and banned

Contrary to what happened in Spain and in Portugal, the *Zensurkammer* (censorship chamber) in the Third Reich felt no need to explain why a work had been forbidden. Therefore, no censorship reports exist. Suppression was even more arbitrary than it might have been in the Iberian Peninsula, where so-called readers had to examine each book or manuscript first and then explain in written form, why they thought it inappropriate for spreading.

In Spain, censorship reports had clear guidelines. To fill out the report, the *lector* (reader in Spanish) had to answer several standard questions.

The leading specialist on the Spanish reports on John Dos Passos is Rosa

Bautista. According to Bautista, Dos Passos's *Manhattan Transfer*, which had been translated by José Robles Pazos, "was first published in Spain in 1929. After a second edition in 1930, there are no traces of further editions until 1960." (2016: 132)

Right after the Spanish Civil War in 1939, the censors of Francisco Franco denied not only the reedition of Spanish translations of the novel but also the import of copies of José Roble's rendition of *Manhattan Transfer*, published in Buenos Aires, Argentina. The censorship report englobes the following questions:

> Is the work against Dogma? Yes. Pages 48, 110, 141
> Against the Church? No.
> Against the Church Ministers? No.
> Against moral principles? Yes. Pages 31, 32, 42, 65, 66, 82, 140, 158, 159, 193, 195, 200, 201, 213, 214, 241, 168, 271, 273, 302, 393, 394.

Against the Regime and its Institutions?
No.
Against persons that have co-operated
with the Regime? No.

Furthermore, the censorship report included a field for commentaries, in which the *lector* noted:

> It is a novel about New York. The whole book is dominated by immorality. Corrupted morals presented naturally in the everyday life of the city. Abortion, adultery, divorce, sodomy, and a variety of [nefarious] sins. (Bautista 2016: 139)

Herewith, the censor concluded that the authorization of the novel had to be denied.

At the risk of being repetitive, it was easier to ban literature under the totalitarian Nazi regime since no explanations had to be produced with which to justify the prohibition, although the responses given by the censor to the inquiries of the Spanish report might be as well, of course, subjective and colored by arbitrariness.

In Portugal, a censorship report had to be produced, too, similar to what happened in Spain; yet, the report contained no rigid guidelines for being filled out. The censorship commission consisted of military personnel of rank, such as captains and lieutenants, who were given the manuscript to read and to decide if it could be authorized for commercialization or if it was to be forbidden and placed on the *Index Librorum Prohibitorum*.

This actually happened to the Brazilian-Portuguese translation of Dos Passos's *Adventures of a Young Man* (*Aventuras de um Comunista*) published in Rio de Janeiro by Guaíra. To be honest, the Brazilian translator changed the title in his translation. *Adventures of a Young Man* became *Adventures of a Communist* in Portuguese. The typewritten report therefore reads: "The title—stupid and contrived—seems to be sheer propaganda, and it aims at being attractive to the masses." Further, the censor wrote, "It's frankly Communist-Marxist [...]. The work is dangerous and seductive to youths. [...] I consider prohibiting the book." (Qtd. in Oliveira 2013: 450)

Nonetheless, a third possibility existed in Portugal. It was possible to authorize the publication 'with cuts,' which essentially meant, that words, sometimes sentences, paragraphs, or whole pages were eliminated from the publication. This, too, happened to Dos Passos.

In 1961, the censorship commission was asked to allow the elaboration of a translation from the French version (note that it was no rendition from the English original) of *Adventures of a Young Man/ Aventures d'un Jeune Homme* translated by Mathilde Camhi. This time the book was authorized, since it was now possible to maintain the exact wording of the original title in the Portuguese translation to be made (*Aventuras dum jovem*) while suppressing those pages that essentially irritated the censor.

> Throughout the book, there are such realistic and crude expressions or words that I think they should be suppressed in the intended translation. [...] These are as follows: 33 - 34 - 55 - 67 - 73 -88 -109 and 310. [...] With these very slight deletions, I believe that the Portuguese translation of this French translation may be authorized. (*Relatório de Censura*: n.p.)

The censor claimed them to be "slight deletions," but the truth was that the novel was being profoundly mutilated.

Mimicry of reality was an annoyance, not only to the Portuguese but also to the German dictator, since the description of reality was thought-provoking and could lead the reader to engage, emending social wrongs that according to the self-pleasing observation of the regime did not exist.

Whereas in Portugal cuts were possible, in Poland and in Italy the translator would take another step forward since he could manipulate all together what was written and how it was written.

> The censor found fault with some parts of Dos Passos's *Manhattan Transfer*. [...] It appears that the censor does not accuse Dos Passos of racism, that he understands the satirical intent, but he writes that 'given the Polish reader' [...] parts of the passage should be [...]

'edited, redrafted'—a commonly used euphemism for censoring.

Herewith the term "kike" was substituted in the Polish translation by the word "Jew" (Looby 2015: 144), whereas the term "chink" was replaced in translation by "Chinese" (Looby 2015: 145), and whenever Congo Jake referred to himself as "nigger," the word would be suppressed and altered in translation, using a politically correct form. That way, "Congo does not use racist words [...] he [...] speaks grammatically, like an educated Pole." (Looby 2015: 192)

As a matter of fact, in Italy almost the same happened under Benito Mussolini. In 1932, the Italian translator of *Manhattan Transfer*, Allesandra Scalero, submitted herself to self-censorship, knowing that otherwise her translation would not have been authorized.

Therefore, in her version of the novel she committed to an "almost systematic expunction of passages dealing with anarchism and its relationship to Italian culture." Of course, "such removals gave way to incongruities in the text." (Iannaccaro 2014: 132) For instance, the Italian character Marco

> could very well be [in the Italian version] either Italian, German, Spanish or Portuguese. [...] Scalero can easily avoid giving any hint of [... Marco's] origins by ennobling his speech and homogenizing it to that of the other characters.

When Marco "predicts an oncoming anarchist revolution [... the] passage is completely excised from the Italian translation." (Iannaccaro 2014: 134-135)

Of course, not only Scalero submitted herself to self-censorship. Cesare Pavese did the same when translating Dos Passos's *The Big Money* into Italian in 1938.

> Pavese made the following comment: [...] I have scrupulously followed the ministry's suggestions, that is, I have anglicized all Italian names, cut all mention of Lenin and the Soviets, deleted or replaced any mention of Fascism, omitted or translated with dignity *wop* or *dago*. (Bonsaver 2007: 139)

These changes, to which Dos Passos's novels were subject in Portugal, Poland, and Italy, occurred unmistakably without the writer's knowledge and consent.

As stated by Kathleen Rommel,

> Dos Passos' personal experience with censorship [included] wartime censorship of correspondence as well as the threat of censorship during publication of his novels because the

author would not 'consent to paraphrases' of his literary work. (2012: xii)

Indeed, Dos Passos had already encountered censorship during his time as an ambulance driver in France and Italy. In a letter he addressed to his friends in the U.S., he had made "anti-war and anti-officialdom remarks." The letter was intercepted through the military mail censor, and Dos Passos was, in consequence, "dishonorably discharged." (Qtd. in Oliveira 2008a: 58)

Furthermore, Dos Passos's manuscript *Three Soldiers* had been rejected thirteen times before it was finally published but "with serious misgivings." (Boyer 2002: 91)

Dos Passos also had to negotiate with Constable, his British publisher, who "wanted to omit the Newsreel and Camera

Eye sections in their edition of *The 42nd Parallel.*" (Ludington 1980: 287) The writer did not condone it.

One might claim that Dos Passos had always "opposed any type of censorship." At all times he "insisted on freedom to publish" what and "wherever he chose." (Willig 1964: 17) When he "published in *The Nation* and the *New Republic*," for example, Dos Passos's "only requirements were that the magazines be free from censorship." (Willig 1964: 10)

Nonetheless, and returning to the point made at the beginning of this argument, the Nazis banned works entirely, with no manipulation of the original, whereas in Portugal, as seen above, cuts, and in Poland, and Italy even the revision of the text were possible.

The reason for preferring to authorize the publication with cuts or with further changes rather than forbidding the work entirely had to do with the fact that these countries did not want people to realize that censorship was so thoroughly exercised. In fact, only the editors and translators would know which parts had been suppressed. The reader of the novel would never become aware of the mutilations of the text.

Even though, as just stressed, no censorship reports were elaborated in Nazi Germany, the *Börsenverein* (German Publishers and Bookseller Association), which now was under the control of the *Reichsschrifttumskammer*, started to send out letters to editors and bookshops, listing names of authors and book titles that they were now forbidding to be printed and sold. Of course, and as seen, no justification was provided. Yet, these lists were "*streng vertraulich*" (strictly confident) and were not allowed to be made publically known. (Balzer 1990: 407) The Nazis feared that the people could use them as bibliographies of must-reads, according to the old proverb: the forbidden fruit is always the sweetest.

Even John Dos Passos was now listed on the "*Börsenblatt* Nr. 112." According to the *Börsenblatt*, "*sämtliche Schriften*" (all writings) by Dos Passos were now forbidden. (Nawrocka 2000: 22)

Fischer, John Dos Passos's German editor, reacted and withdrew temporarily its author's books from the market. Nevertheless, Fischer decided soon after to re-offer and re-sell Dos Passos's German translations, since the American writer had been "mistakenly" placed on the black list because foreign writers had not yet officially been dealt with by the *Reichsschrifttumskammer*. (Cf. Nawrocka 2000: 23)

The priority of the Nazis was to purge all German literature first and only then, and on separate lists, the works of foreign writers, as it was the case of John Dos Passos.

For the Nazis, foreign literature did actually not exist. According to their racist dogma, a piece of writing had to be produced in German to be considered literature. If it was written in a foreign language, it was looked down on. Therefore, the Nazis despised John Dos Passos, anyway, because he was not German but *Luso*-American, writing in English and not in German, to them the only real and superior language that could generate a work of art.

Yet, despite this prejudiced deduction, John Dos Passos was in truth a celebrity in Germany.

In 1931, Werner Neuse wrote his Ph.D. at the University of Gießen on Dos Passos's literary progress and career.

Famous writers like Bertold Brecht, Erich Kästner, and Kurt Tucholsky, among many other contemporaries, had read Dos Passos and spoke highly of his talent. Under the pseudonym Peter Panter, Kurt Tucholsky wrote a book review in 1928 for the *Weltbühne* on *Manhattan Transfer*, referring as well to *Three Soldiers*:

> There is *Manhattan Transfer* by John Dos Passos (S. Fischer in Berlin). This half-American, whose *Three Soldiers* (Malik *Verlag*) is not enough recommended, has done something good. [...] *Manhattan Transfer* is a good book [...]. These are photographs, no, actually these are really good little etchings that are shown to us; If they are real, I cannot judge, the people who lived long enough over there, say yes. Within it is the poetry of the big city; it is a thoroughly masculine lyric. [...] Dos Passos is not only a poet, but also a gifted writer. The translation of *Manhattan Transfer* by Paul Baudisch is clean and decent. (1928: 287)

The German translation of *Three Soldiers* (*Drei Soldaten*) had been written by Julian Gumperz for the Malik *Verlag* that published the novel in 1922. Paul Baudisch's translation of *Manhattan Transfer, der Roman einer Stadt* (the novel of a city) with a preface by Sinclair Lewis came out five years later and was published by Fischer. Baudisch further rendered *The 42nd Parallel* (*Der 42. Breitengrad*) into German, which had been released in 1930. Besides, he translated *Nineteen Nineteen* (*Auf den Trümern, Roman zweier Kontinente—On the ruins, a novel of two continents*) for Fischer, which appeared in 1932.

When the first German edition of *Three Soldiers* sold out, the Malik *Verlag* reproduced the novel's translation in 1932. Another print came out in 1935, at a time when Dos Passos's books had already been burned by the students and the *Börsenblatt* had wrongly blacklisted the writer.

Actually, it was only on December 31, 1938—almost three years later—that John Dos Passos's entire work was officially forbidden from circulating in the Third Reich. The entry this time correctly listed in the "*Verzeichnis englischer und nordamerikanischer Schriftsteller*" (Directory of English and North-American writers) simply read: "Surname: Dos Passos; First given name: John Roderigo; Title: entire work." (1938: 27)

From this point forward, the edict was sternly to be executed. The remaining works of the writer were immediately removed from public libraries, and Dos Passos's editors were prohibited from selling or reprinting his works. Existing copies had to be destroyed.

Any forbidden writer was automatically declared *persona non grata*, which meant that John Dos Passos could no longer visit Germany. In comparison, Dos Passos, of whom some works had been forbidden in the Portuguese *Estado Novo* (New State, 1933 – 1974)—as António de Oliveira Salazar's dictatorship was called— could nevertheless travel freely through Portugal, which Dos Passos actually did on July 20, 1960, when he visited with his family Madeira Island. Ironically, Dos Passos was even honored by the President of the Municipal Chamber, Sequeira Cabrita, in Ponta do Sol, for his achievements in world literature. A commemoration plaque was placed at the façade of the house that belonged to Dos Passos's forbearers. In the Third Reich, however, the ban was impermissible.

Two German translators of John Dos Passos's did not wait for their author to be banned. They early decided, almost immediately after the *Machtergreifung*, to leave Germany.

Julian Gumperz, who had been born in New York but had lived in Germany ever since he studied in Frankfurt, had been a communist activist. He had also been one of the shareholders of the leftist Malik *Verlag* that published Dos Passos. After the Nazis closed down the Institute for Social Research, where Gumperz worked, he returned to the USA, eventually finding a teaching position at the prestigious Columbia University. Like Dos Passos in his later years, Gumperz, toward the end of his life, rather disappointedly distanced himself from the left.

Baudisch, who was a writer in his own right—he had written plays and novels such as *Familie Mächtig* (*The mighty family*), *Schlumpf oder das groteske Pathos* (*Schlumpf or the grotesque Pathos*), *Passion*, and *Der Zeitgeist*—had been a party member of the KPD (*Kommunistische Partei Deutschlands*—German Communist Party). He too feared for his safety in Nazi Germany and decided to leave. First he left for Austria, living in his place of birth, Vienna, but when the country was annexed by the Nazis in 1938, Baudisch had to flee again, this time to Paris and eventually to Stockholm, where he went on living as a translator, screenplay writer, and song text writer.

The annexation of Austria meant, of course, that the National-Socialist censorship was also introduced to the country and that from now on the *Reichsschrifttumskammer* in Berlin was in charge. Books forbidden in Germany were prohibited in Austria, too, which applied as well to the writings of John Dos Passos.

Yet, not only Dos Passos's translators fled the country. Also, John Heartfield (pseudonym for Helmut Herzfeld), the famous German artist, who had authored for the Malik *Verlag* in 1922 the cover of the German rendition of *Three Soldiers*, left the Third Reich in December 1933, right after the S.A. had searched his house.

Heartfield became famous for his photomontage: "*Der Sinn des Hitlergrußes, Kleiner Mann bittet um große Gaben. Motto: Millionen stehen hinter mir!*" (The significance behind the Hitler salute: Little man asks for big contributions. Motto: Millions stand behind me!), published in 1932, showing Adolf Hitler raising his hand for the Nazi salute, receiving from behind, and on the palm of his outstretched hand, a bunch of banknotes. Besides referring to Hitler as a little man, Heartfield accused, with his photomontage, the *Führer* of being greedy and that not millions of people stood behind him but a few of the corrupting rich.

Having criticized the *Führer* in this way and fearing persecution, Heartfield decided to flee to Prague, once the Nazis came to power. There, Heartfield went on working as an artist. Right after the book burning took place in Berlin, he published the cover: "*Durch Licht zur Nacht*" (Through light to the night) for the *Arbeiter-Illustrierte-Zeitung* (*Workers Illustrated Newspaper*) that exposed Joseph Goebbels with his index finger raised in front of the burning *Reichstag* (German Parliament) with a collage of the *auto-de-fé*.

In 1938, Heartfield had to flee once more from the Nazis, this time to the United Kingdom, right after the German invasion of Czechoslovakia. In the UK, Heartfield was suspected and treated as an enemy alien and was interned in a detention camp.

In the early 1950's, Heartfield returned to Germany, living henceforth until his death in the German Democratic Republic.

The new literature under the swastika

Banning literature of world relevance, on the one hand, the Nazis promoted a 'new' type of literature, on the other, which they referred to as *Blut und Boden Literatur* (blood and soil literature), *Heimatliteratur* (homeland literature), and *Weihedichtung* (literature of consecration).

These new literary movements clearly contrasted with John Dos Passos's views and his perception of fiction. Whereas Dos Passos approached his creative writing as a "contemporary chronicle" (Oliveira 2013: 468), and thus as a historical account of events, the aim of the new National-Socialist literature was to install faith in the Nazi ideology and generate followers if necessary by creating 'alternative facts.'

Books were supposed to carry and support pleasingly Nazi propaganda.

Murder was to be made reputable. History was to be rewritten by creating and disseminating conspiracy theories, such as the *Dolchstoßlegende* (stab-in-the-back myth) that aimed at blaming Social-Democrats for Germany's loss of WWI. Literature became therefore a mediator of deception and not of the truth.

To implement these goals, the *Reichsschrifttumskammer* craved for and sanctioned the *Blut und Boden Literatur*, which essentially consisted of war and peasant novels.

Concerning the first mentioned, their authors had to glorify and idealize the war. Their characters were soldiers that were expected to be described as courageous, and ready to sacrifice their lives for their patria. Their deaths were referred to as the *Heldentod* (heroic death).

Moreover, the soldiers in these novels had to be characterized as being unconditionally obedient, unquestioning, and unthinking.

Between officers of rank and ordinary privates, comradery had to be stressed, as well as the right of the strongest to rule the conquered territory.

A clear perception of the enemy, who, of course, was the only one committing atrocities during wartime, and whose race was seen as inferior and unworthy, had to be worked out, too.

Marching songs within the novels served to create and stress the camaraderie, in which the individual passed through the process of depersonalization to become one with his military unit. (See Wilpert 1989: 609)

These novels essentially served a purpose, since they aimed at emerging within the German people the readiness to fight and to die for their country in the case of war.

One of the exponents of these war novels was Ernst Jünger with *In Stahlgewittern* (*Storm of Steel*), published in 1920, portraying the war as a purifying force and as part of human nature.

Ernst Jünger, who volunteered during WWI, wrote:

> Suddenly Gipkens [who commanded the company] seized hold of me and pulled me to one side. Next moment a shot flew into splinters on the very place where I had been sitting. By a lucky chance he had seen a rifle barrel slowly pushed forward out of a loophole in the block only forty meters from us. The keen eye of an artist had saved my life. (Jünger 1996: 293)

The cited text shows an officer saving the life of one of his men. By describing the officer's eyesight as that of an artist,

Jünger intended to exalt his soldiery skills, whereas, the fact that the enemy shooter doesn't show himself openly (only the barrel of his shotgun is visible) stresses the sneakiness and shadiness of the enemy.

Jünger also intended to depict the normalcy of war life;

> In the afternoon I was tempted from my coalhole by some not particularly violent artillery fire, though I was at the moment comfortably reading, over a cup of coffee. (Jünger 1996: 293)

The character is represented to have no fear; he is reading "comfortably," a rather odd word that you wouldn't expect to find in a war novel, and he drinks coffee, as if war were an ordinary, everyday life situation.

Another character in the novel was wounded. He had "a splinter in his back," and he fortified himself with "a pull at the bottle." No pain is described, but the heroism of men, who do not complain and bear their destiny and even wounded go on fighting, whereas the "English [enemies flee] to a line behind." (Jünger 1996: 295-6)

One of the chapters in *Storm of Steel* ends with the words:

> In particular, Lieutenant Jünger earned fresh recognition. Already six times wounded, he was on the occasion, as always, a shining example to both officers and men. (Jünger 1996: 299)

Again, being wounded is depicted as a form of honor and bravery that makes Jünger (himself the main character in his novel) shine and be distinguished among other soldiers.

Many of his teen and adolescent readers dreamed of being likewise distinguished with the *Eiserne Kreuz* (Iron Cross—Medal of Honor). Such descriptions awakened their willingness to become soldiers themselves, to fight, and to die for the *Vaterland* (fatherland).

The German-speaking writer Ödön von Horváth soon became aware of this distorted eagerness of the *Kriegsroman* (war novel); in *Jugend ohne Gott* (*Youth without God*), a novel on the misguided Hitler Youth, which Horváth published in 1937, he wrote critically, "They'd die on a battlefield! To have their name on some war memorial that's the dream of their puberty." (Horváth 2012: 28)

Another writer of war novels was Hans Grimm. In 1926, Grimm had published *Volk ohne Raum* (*People without space*), in which he advocated for the expansion of the German Reich and encouraged war action. Very much in line with the Nazis, Grimm claimed that the German people needed more arable land and had to conquer new territories.

As stated before, John Dos Passos did not fit into this category. With his anti-war novel *Three Soldiers*,[9] he had made a clear statement that war was cruel and horrible, but in no way heroic. One of the main characters of *Three Soldiers*, John Andrews, opposes vehemently "the drill and the meaninglessness of the war." (Oliveira, 2010: 199) Andrews is wounded and hospitalized and becomes

> a victim of the most intense mental agony [...] he knows also the greatest physical pain. His first hope, after the first wild hours of pain, [...] is that he will be discharged from the army to 'live' again. (Allen 1966: 30)

---

[9] In 1922, previously to *Three Soldiers*, Dos Passos had written the anti-war novel *One Man's Initiation, 1917*; yet this novel was not as notorious compared to *Three Soldiers* and thus had not been translated by then into German.

In Dos Passos's novel, there are no traces of heroism after a soldier's wounding. Neither is there in Andrews the wish to die courageously for the great cause. To the contrary, Andrews refers to the war as a senseless "butchery," and instead of obeying orders, he deserts the army in the end. (Allen 1966: 30)

Camaraderie among ordinary soldiers and their higher-ups—a requisition of the Nazi war novel—does not even occur in Dos Passos's *Three Soldiers*. The character Eisenstein, for instance, is "put aside by his whole company" (Oliveira 2010: 199), whereas Chrisfield, another character of the novel, "kills his sergeant, who constantly commands him around." (Oliveira 2013: 451) Finally, the soldier Dan Fuselli is treated unfairly, and never gets promoted to corporal. (Oliveira 2013: 271)

The second type of literary movement saluted by the Nazis, previously referred to as soil literature or *Heimatliteratur*, had to exalt life on the countryside and was expected to approve of the Nazi morals.

One of the most important figures of the *Heimatroman* (homeland novel) was the mother that was to be rendered as "*Hüterin der Rasse*" (guardian of the [German] race). Of course, the mother had to be blond and blue-eyed, and had to epitomize the female representative of the Aryan race. In alignment with the Nazi mentality, any female character was expected to give birth, love and nurture her children and husband, cook, and take care of the household and the children's education in the novel's plot. There was no place for women's emancipation.

Men had to be described as blond, too, and muscled. They were depicted as hardworking farmers. Referring back to the

Germanic cult, a simplistic life in a close bond to nature, plowing the land, was idealized. Like the Germanic tribe in ancient times, the German people were supposed to live from agriculture and re-establish a profound connection with their local traditions and their village community. Literature was intended to communicate to its readers the new German values that dated back to the old, original morals of the Germanic clans.

In her children's book *Mutter, erzähl von Adolf Hitler* (*Mother tell me about Adolf Hitler*), Johanna Haarer, a German medical doctor, collected several fairy tales, illustrated by Rolf Winkler, whose story titles say it all: "*Adolf Hitler sorgt für Arbeit und Brot,*" (Adolf Hitler provides work and bread), "*Adolf Hitler lindert die Not in Deutschland,*" (Adolf Hitler alleviates the need in Germany), and "*Adolf Hitler hilft den Bauern*" (Adolf

Hitler helps the peasants). This last story begins with the words:

> "Do you know another story like the one about the people from the Thuringian Forest, mother?" The children came in from playing outside. "A story in which everything turned out all right in the end, because Adolf Hitler helped us again, yes?" said the mother, smiling. Let me think.—Yes, I know one! And the children pulled up their chairs and hurried to make sure that each of them had a good seat next to their mother. (Haarer 1939: 164)

The story that the mother tells her children is, much to the delight of the Nazis, about a peasant family, whose father and sons worked hard in the fields, while the mother took care of the household, sweeping the floor, making the beds, and taking care of the pigs and the chickens.

When their father died, the eldest son inherited the farm. But one of the younger brothers wanted some farmland for himself, too.

So one day, the youngest brother went to town, where he met a Jew, who told him that according to the law, the farm had to be divided equally among all the heirs.

In the story, the Jew is described as "small [...] with black, frizzy hair and a crooked nose." (Haarer 1939: 169) He is further referred to by the narrator as a "devil." (Haarer 1939: 170)

In addition, the Jew was portrayed as manipulative; he gave the youngest brother some alcohol, to cloud his mind, so that he would eventually confront his elder brother and demand his share of the farm.

From that day on, the eldest brother felt threatened that the division of the fields would not leave enough arable land for each of the brothers and that none of them would be able to feed their families.

The story ends with the words "Since Adolf Hitler is our *Führer*, the Jews have nothing more to say or to decide in Germany." (Haarer 1939: 175)

Once again, Hitler is presented as the savior. According to the narrator of the story, he saved this poor family from its plight by changing the laws.

In fact, in September 1933, the Nazis introduced the *Reichserbhofgesetz* (Heritage Farm Act of the Reich) which declared:

> Farms are to be protected from over-indebtedness and fragmentation of inheritance, so that they remain in the hands of free farmers in perpetuity. (Nicolai 2010: 36)

However, the Jew who is blamed in the 'fairy tale' had nothing to do with the previous law that allowed the division of arable land among all heirs. The 'damnable' law had been passed in the *Reichstag* (parliament) by its members, not by the Jew, who is once again being used as a scapegoat for all social ills.

As said above, the *Bauerndichtung* (peasant literature) rendered life in the countryside rather positively, while, contrariwise, it demonized modern city life. (Note that the Jew in Johanna Haarer's story came from the 'dreadful' town.)

People in the cities lived individualistically and had a tendency to become both overly intellectualized and internationalized, which was seen by the Nazis as the source of all evil. In the corrupted cities, the Nazis accused, the people had become uprooted and had lost the bonds with nature and their supportive clan. Their lives had become unnatural.

Among the exponents of the new *Heimatliteratur* were Agnes Miegel, Hanns Johst, and Will Vesper. Paradoxically, the majority among these authors had been brought up in the cities and never really had lived in a village. (See Wilpert 1989: 82)

Again, John Dos Passos did not blend in; his *Großstadtroman* (novel of the metropolis), *Manhattan Transfer*, was called by the Nazis disapprovingly *Asphaltliteratur* (asphalt literature). It portrayed the hectic and chaotic life in the metropolis. The countryside is almost completely left out of its scope.

For the Nazis, Dos Passos's characters lived abnormally, since they had lost all bonds with nature. They had modern, stressful employments, and their families disintegrated.

Many of Dos Passos's female characters, such as Margo Dowling, who lived apart from her husband and became a movie actress in *The Big Money*, may stand as the archetype of a modern emancipated woman, loathed by the Nazis.

Furthermore, John Dos Passos's modernist novel contained social criticism that the Nazis did not welcome. All criticism contained thought-provoking impulses. But the Nazis did not want the people to think. The aim was to educate them to follow orders without questioning; yet, criticism implied making interrogations. What the Nazis wanted was that authors celebrated the beautiful, harmonious, ideal world on the countryside, where there was no stress and where family life was still intact and unspoiled, creating an illusion of a homogenous, perfect, faultless, and therefore utopian society.

In addition, Dos Passos portrayed the internationalization of New York; among the many immigrants that appear in *Manhattan Transfer* is the character Congo Jake, who becomes wealthy through bootlegging. By introducing immigrants to his novel, Dos Passos creates a heterogenic, pluralistic view of New York. The Nazis went passionately against immigration. According to them, only Germans were to live and thrive in the Third Reich. Immigration was not to be positively referred to in literature; neither was society intended to be educated to open-mindedness, which again clashed with Dos Passos's personal views.

Finally, there was the so-called *Weihedichtung*, which almost prophetically hailed the *Führer*, the fatherland, and the Nazi flag. These odes to Adolf Hitler had a religious quality in them, professing the author's utmost belief that the *Führer* would bring blessings to the country. Among the authors of the *Weihedichtung*, were Heinrich Anacker, Gerhard Schumann, and Herybert Menzel. (See Hertbruggen 2019: 213)

Also, Baldur von Schirach, the *Reichsjugendführer* (*Führer* of the Hitler Youth), had written a poem that was put to music by Hans Otto-Borgmann and soon became the hymn of the Nazi youth organization. The text, composed in the style of the *Weihedichtung,* read:

> Our flag flutters before us.
> Into the future we march man for man
> We march for Hitler
> Through night and through hardship
> With the banner of youth
> For freedom and bread.
>
> Our flag flutters before us,
> Our flag is the new era.
> And the flag leads us into eternity!

Yes, the flag is more than death!

Youth! Youth!
We are soldiers of the future.
Youth! Youth!
Bearers of the deeds to come.
Yes, through our fists will fall
Those who oppose us

Youth! Youth!
We are soldiers of the future.
Youth! Youth!
Bearers of the deeds to come.
Führer, we belong to you...
(Lamprecht 2015: 7)[10]

The poem undeniably celebrates soldiery, the flag, and the *Führer*, and it asserts the promise of a new era of abundance.

---

[10] Today this song is forbidden in Germany. It may not be sung publically and it may be quoted for educational purposes only.

Instead of professing that Hitler was a blessing for Germany, John Dos Passos was actually a harsh critic of the dictator. In his article "Thank you Mr. Hitler," published in *Common Sense* in April 27, 1933, Dos Passos mockingly stated:

> That continent, between the false mustache of the Jew-baiter Hitler and Mussolini's castor oil squint, has sunk back to the cultural level of the Thirty Years War. (1933: 13)

"Thank you Mr. Hitler" questioned if the "recent development in Germany," that is, the *Machtergreifung* by the National-Socialist movement, would be thinkable in America. Dos Passos gave "warning," that according to his viewpoint, a "Brown Shirt movement" was possible in the U.S., too. He wrote:

A good whang on the back of the head from a polieman's night-stick will often give a man a sense of reality that nothing else will. That is, if it doesn't knock him clean out of his wits. The events now taking place in Germany should give a salutary awakening jolt to all Americans whose lives do not directly depend on the exploiting of their fellowmen. [...] The owning and exploiting groups in Germany, in this case the industrialists and the [...] landwoners, found that the exploited were getting a little too powerful [... so] they rigged this pretty little Nazi picnic for them. [...] Our owners and exploiters, our bankers and power magnates will gladly do the same thing [...]. The men on top have minds geared only for profit, for their own power and easy money. (1933: 13)

John Dos Passos, as many historians (and the artist John Heartfield with his "*Der Sinn des Hitlergrußes*"), claimed that the Nazi government had been predominantly sponsored by rich businessmen. It was only in the 1970's that the American historian Henry Ashby Turner denied and corrected these false assertions. His studies proved that the majority of the industrials in Germany were all but pleased with the rise of Hitler and had neither subsidized nor backed the NSDAP during the elections. To tell the truth, it had been predominantly the ordinary German people, who had sponsored Hitler. (See Turner 1980: 10)

Somewhat predictably, many German readers did not find the officially endorsed types of literature appealing, as they lacked quality and depth. Since all writers of eminence had been silenced through censorship, the German classics like Johann Wolfgang von Goethe and Friedrich von Schiller figured as the best-sellers of these days, even though one of Schiller's most famous plays, *Wilhelm Tell*, had been forbidden by the Nazis, too, since it was a "*Freiheitsstück*" (play on freedom).

In the plot, Tell, who was a hunter and a good archer, refused to greet properly the bailiff Gessler, who then forced Tell to shoot an apple from his son's head. Schiller portrayed Gessler as a tyrant avid for power, whose description might have resembled Hitler's despotism in many regards. In the end, Tell killed Gessler.

Being a play on freedom, and given that tyranny lost in the end, the play could not have been recommended by the regime. Actually, all texts that supported freedom and were pro-democratic were barred—another reason for the Nazis to gag Dos Passos, who had always come out in defense of liberty, as clearly stated, amongst others, in Dos Passos's *The Theme Is Freedom*, where the author, for instance, regretted "Franco's victory" in Spain that "encouraged Hitler to engage in new adventures to subvert the peace and freedom of Europe." (Dos Passos 1956: 151)

Moreover, texts that were considered *Judaica* of all sorts, i.e., books[11] that were written by Jews or by people of Jewish ancestry, were outlawed. All texts that diluted racism and anti-Semitism or that pled for integration were *verboten* (forbidden).

John Dos Passos was severely against any form of anti-Semitism. In *Manhattan*

---

[11] In fact, not only books were banned. *Frakturschrift* (a font consisting of broken letters), which had been widely used by the Nazis until the early 1940s, was considered to have been created by Jews. The *Judenletters*, as the Nazis came to refer to them derogatorily, were outlawed on January 3, 1941, and were to be replaced by Antiqua. Ironically, *Fraktur* was not developed by Jews at all. Therefore, banning *Fraktur* may have served another purpose. The font was difficult to decipher. You had to get used to reading it. After invading several countries, it became necessary for the Nazis to use a font that the people in those territories could read effortlessly so that they could comply with the Nazis' orders.

Transfer, his character Jimmy Herf feels uneasy when he is forced by circumstances to listen to his uncle Jeff speaking pejoratively of the New Yorker Jews;

> New York [..] is no longer what it used to be [...]. City's overrun with kikes and low Irish, that's what's the matter with it... [...] After all we built up this country and then we allow a lot of foreigners, the scum of Europe, the offscourings of Polish ghettos to come and run it for us. [...] And add to that the ignorance of these dirty kikes and shanty Irish that we make voters before they can even talk English. [...] Jimmy sat in his chair with pins and needles in his legs. (1986: 99-100)

Furthermore, John Dos Passos referred to the popularity of the jazz in his works, a type of music the Nazis banned in all public spaces, labeling it derogatively the "Nigger-Jazz." The Nazis ended its radiophonic broadcast in 1935. To replace it, they suggested the music of the anti-Semite composer Richard Wagner, whose *Rienzi der Letzte Tribun* (*Rienzi the Last of the Tribunes*) was actually Adolf Hitler's favorite opera. Also, *Konzertmusik* (concert music) by the composer Richard Strauss (who headed the *Reichsmusik-kammer* from 1933 onwards), *Volksmusik* (traditional music), and *Militärmusik* (military music) became popular by compulsion.

Concerning African-Americans, John Dos Passos explored discrimination in his novels, condemning prejudice. The character Janey in *U.S.A.*, for example, is forbidden by her mother to play with an African-American girl named Pearl; Janey ends up crying because she does not understand her mother's defense of segregation;

One afternoon [Janey] asked Pearl to come in and they played dolls together [...] in the back yard. When Pearl had gone Mommer's voice called from the kitchen. [...] "Yes, Mommer." [...] "Jane, I want to talk to you about something. That little colored girl you brought in this afternoon..." Janey's heart was dropping. She had a sick feeling and felt herself blushing [... "You] mustn't bring that little colored girl in the house again. [... You] must never associate with colored people on an equal basis. [...]." Janey tried to speak but she couldn't. She stood stiff in the middle of the yard [...]." Janey began to cry. (Qtd. in Oliveira 2013: 267-268)

The Nazis had no compassion for other races, especially not for Jews and Black people. The new Nazi literature was requested to expose both Jewish and Black people, unfavorably and always as inferior and as criminals. Dos Passos, however, did the contrary. In *Manhattan Transfer*, for instance, a pyromaniac is definitely white and not black; yet, despite this fact, a Black man is ridiculously being accused of the felony:

> Witnesses describe a firebug as being male and 'pale.' But the police arrest no man that would have matched to the poor description of the offender, but a 'negro,' who they accused of the delinquencies. Being dark-skinned, the African American man could have hardly been the crook. [... It] seems unlikely that the police, by this time anxious to arrest someone for the series of fires, have found the culprit in the black man. The significance of this mistake is compounded by the police officer's brutal treatment of the suspect—'whose arms snap [...] back and forth like broken cables' as three of them 'crack [...] the negro first on one side of the head, then on the other' with billy clubs. (Nanney 1998: 164)

There was still another reason for antagonizing John Dos Passos. Early in his life, the writer had come out in defense of several anarchists, such as the young poet David Gordon, the factory worker Nicola Sacco and the fish-peddler Bartolomeo Vanzetti, as well as the editor and publisher of *Il Martello* (*The Hammer*) Carlo Tresca. All of them, Dos Passos accused, had been wrongly convicted for the crimes of being foreigners and of expressing themselves freely, according to their political beliefs.

In 1927, David Gordon had been

> sentenced to three years in the city reformatory because his poem, published in the *Daily Worker* [on March 12, 1927], was considered "obscene." Yet, for Dos Passos it was clear that in truth "the boy's real crime [...] was that he was writing for a communist publication and that he was a Russian Jew." The

obscenity of the poem was certainly in its savage criticism of America, already outlined in its opening verses: "America is a land of censored opportunity/ Lick spit; eat dirt,/ There's your opportunity; [...]/ You're everything aren't you America?/ Of course/ You're even a neat whore house/ [...] Two dollars a woman:/ Nice bed/ Warm room./ But most important:/ A fleshy woman." The poem stressed that America had betrayed its dream. America promised to its immigrants opportunities, but what they found when they arrived was a life without dignity. The immigrant performed odd jobs. Love did not exist; prostitution did. Worst of all, Americans were proud of it, and thought of themselves as morally superior to other people. Dos Passos defended much the same line of thought at the time as David Gordon. A petition was signed by approximately three hundred supporters that asked for Gordon's release, among them intellectuals with international renown such as Max Eastman, and

Heywood Broun, who found the "draconian sentence in his newspaper column 'a piece of judicial folly.'" John Dos Passos tried to convince F. Scott Fitzgerald to come to public to speak up for Gordon, too. He sent him a letter, which summarized the case. It read: "the Daily Worker was prosecuted [...] for publishing a poem supposed to be obscene by David Gordon, a boy of eighteen, at present holding a [Zona Gale literary] scholarship [...] at the University Wisconsin. Gordon and the Daily Worker were found guilty of violating section 1141 of the Penal Law. David Gordon was sentenced to [a] term at the City Reformatory. [...] Three years of the company of young criminals of every description, of beating by prison guards, a grim substitute for the college education he had earned by his obvious precocious talent as a writer. He is at present serving his term at the Reformatory. If you read the enclosed excerpts from the remarks of the judges you will understand the atmosphere of

meanness and spite that surrounded the trial. The boy's real crime was that he was writing for a communist publication and that he was a Russian Jew. If this is the penalty for obscenity and disgust with America, most of our best writers should be in jail at this moment. The important thing now is not to complain about fair play or freedom of speech, but to get him out. [...] Please write at once."
In the end—due to the public pressure—Gordon had only to serve one month in prison; eventually he was re-admitted to University. (Qtd. in Oliveira 2013: 186)

America promoted itself as the land of freedom and opportunity; and yet, this freedom to express oneself and the opportunity to thrive and live in dignity had been denied to many. In the case of David Gordon, the youngster had been censored and punished for his boldness to speak his mind, and John Dos Passos worried and contested this form of brutal censorship.

Concerning Sacco and Vanzetti, they had been accused of robbery and murder. Yet, proof was very flimsy. Nevertheless, both men were sentenced to death. For Dos Passos, the trial had been unfair, and Sacco and Vanzetti had been condemned because they were foreign anarchists rather than being guilty of assault or manslaughter. Dos Passos "wrote sarcastically, 'If two Italians are spreading anarchist propaganda, you hold them for murder.'" (Qtd. in Oliveira 2013: 180) Dos Passos's further explained:

> When we took up for Sacco and Vanzetti we were taking up for freedom of speech and for an evenhanded judicial system which would give the same treatment to poor men as to rich men, to greasy foreigners as to redblooded Americans. (Qtd. in Oliveira 2013: 174)

Yet, freedom of speech had been denied to Sacco and Vanzetti as well as their right to life. They had been politically censored and therefore murdered in the land of liberty, prospect, peace, and plenty, as the American myth ironically proclaimed, a fact that the young David Gordon also critically assessed in his poem partially quoted above.

Besides John Dos Passos had also come in defense of Carlo Tresca, who had been silenced in 1923 by prosecution for his publication of *Il Martello*

> an Italian-language radical periodical published in New York. *Il Martello* was suppressed ostensibly because of some advertisement for birth-control books, but in reality because the Italian ambassador to the United States had publicly complained about Tresca's vigorous stand against Mussolini. (Boyer 2002: 241)

Tresca was murdered on January 1, 1943. His death meant a great loss to Dos Passos, who not only had defended Tresca but had also become his friend. Dos Passos dedicated Tresca an obituary in *The Theme Is Freedom* and turned him into the character Nick Pignatelli in *Chosen Country* and into Ugo Salvatore in Dos Passos's posthumously published *Century's Ebb*.

The Nazis were far-right extremists; no literature was allowed that revealed sympathy or came out in defense of leftist concerns, parties, movements or individuals. Thus by speaking on behalf of Gordon, Sacco and Vanzetti, and Tresca, Dos Passos had crossed the line; at least from the Nazi point of view. Tresca's criticism of Mussolini, a fellow fascist, was similarly perceived as harmful and destructive, adding to the Nazis' contempt for Dos Passos.

Last but not least, the Nazis accused John Dos Passos of being immoral since he used slang and swear words in his fiction. In *Adventures of a Young Man*, for instance, Dos Passos wrote:

> "Come in Toby, you old c—r ... Jesus Christ it does me good to see you."
> "Well, Duke, you old son of a bitch, what do you think of the nation's capital?"
> "Aw, shit..." (1967: 31)

Even though Dos Passos self-censors himself with the c-word, he uses the interjection "Jesus Christ," uttered as an exclamation of surprise, and the expression "son of a bitch," as well as the word "shit" in his novel.

For the Nazis, literature had to be pure. Characters were not supposed to be vulgar, under any circumstances, even if they were country boys, with a low level of education, and therefore would most likely make use of foul language in real life.

For the Nazis, literature was not supposed to be a mirror of society as intended by John Dos Passos. Literature was expected to teach people the new German values. After that, literature only served the function of being entertaining and to create a fictional world of perfection and faultlessness, so that the people could forget about their own problems and their own miseries for a few moments, as long as their reading lasted.

Homelessness
and speechlessness

Many of the writers who remained in Germany and did not condescend to create as they were expected to do, were expelled to go on writing (*Berufsverbot*— occupational ban) just like Erich Kästner, while others, like Kästner's illustrator Erich Ohser,[12] author of the famous *Vater Sohn*

---

[12] The Nazis not only burned books but also works of art. On March 10, 1939, they cynically chose Berlin's fire department to publically burn more than 5,000 paintings, aquarelles, sculptures, and drawings. This fact actually influenced Ray Bradbury's dystopia *Fahrenheit 451*, first published in 1953. Among the authors that the Nazis despised as *entartete Kunst* (degenerated art) were Otto Dix, Paul Klee, Emil Nolde, Wassily Kandinsky, Marc Chagall, and George Grosz. The latter left Germany in 1932 and settled in the U.S., a fact that went not unnoticed by John Dos Passos. He considered "George Grosz, the great visual satirist of our time," and welcomed that the modernist artist had "come to live" in the U.S. and even had "taken out papers and [considered] himself an American." This, Dos

Bildergeschichten (*Father-Son* picture stories), was imprisoned, after his neighbor denounced Ohser for criticizing the regime. Ohser (who used the pen name e. o. plauen to avoid the occupational ban) committed suicide in his cell, whereas his friend, the German writer and journalist Erich Knauf, who had also been imprisoned, was beheaded for disdainfully mocking the *Führer*. The Nazis were cruel enough to send the bill of Knauf's execution to his wife, Erna Donath.

Carl von Ossietzky was also punished with *Publikationsverbot* (interdiction of publishing). The famous writer was imprisoned and transported to the concentration camp Sonnenburg, where he was forced to carry out the heavy work in the moors, until he got severely sick. Even though Ossietzky was released from the

---

Passos wrote, made him "feel good about" the United States. (2003: 613)

Konzentrationslager (extermination camp) because he had in the meantime been nominated for the Nobel Prize in Literature, he was held in arrest in a sanatorium near Berlin. Hitler promised him release and a pension if he renounced the prize that had been awarded to Ossietzky for his sharp criticism against the Nazi regime. Ossietzky refused. Hitler reacted with rage, forbidding any German to henceforth receive the Nobel Prize in whichever category. Sadly enough, Ossietzky died shortly afterwards, in 1938.

The majority of writers became afraid of the Nazis; they feared for their lives and chose to leave the Third Reich and to live from now on in exile. By leaving, the writers automatically lost their German citizenship.

Thomas Mann, for instance, was listed in the *Ausbürgerungsliste* (list of expatriation) that appeared in the

Reichsanzeiger (*Reich's Gazette*), which not only meant that he had lost his nationality but that his properties and possessions in Germany had been confiscated as well. (Schröter 1998: 111)

Lion Feuchtwanger fled to France. And yet a group of Stormtroopers invaded his home in Grunewald and smashed Feuchtwanger's furniture. His servants were brutally beaten up. Also in Feuchtwanger's case, his assets were seized and he was stripped of the doctor title that he received from the University of Munich. (See Wagener 1996: 47)

Even though these intellectuals were being harassed and persecuted in Germany, some countries denied them entry because they feared these writers would abuse their welfare system (see Schlosser 1994: 257), and later, when the Second World War broke out, because they perceived them as enemy aliens.

Between 1933 and 1938, many of these exiles stayed in Germany's neighboring countries. But with the annexation of Austria, and later on the occupation of France and other European countries, things changed. They had to flee once again.

The Soviet Union opened its doors to German writers, but only if the latter could proof that they had sympathized with communism or that they had been members of the KPD.

Besides being a famous leftist author, Johannes R. Becher had been affiliated with the German Communist Party, and thus his plea to settle in the Soviet Union had been accepted.

Switzerland was a neutral country, and many writers stayed there for some time. But being expensive for living, many among the exiled, like Bertold Brecht, decided to move elsewhere, in Brecht's case eventually to the United States.

Writing in German but living in other countries, where German was not spoken, meant as a last consequence to abandon their once promising careers as writers. This meant that they now suffered from both "*Heimatlosigkeit*" (homelessness), on the one hand, and "*Sprachlosigkeit*" (speechlessness), on the other. As a matter of fact, only those who already had been internationally famous before they fled from Germany were able to continue to survive as novelists. (Schlosser 1994: 255)

Dos Passos's banning in Nazi Germany meant for him being robbed of a considerable part of royalties, but to be honest, he did not go bankrupt, nor was he inhibited to go on living as a writer, unlike his German colleagues.

To overcome their speechlessness, many started to learn English, such as

Theodor Czokor and Ödön von Horváth; nonetheless, the latter was, as he expressed, "ungifted for foreign languages," giving up the attempt in the end. (Krischke 1998b: 185)

In the receiving countries, these German writers now tried to found clubs and associations that would organize concerts, exhibitions, and meetings. But they also tried to find publishers willing to print their works in German. Emanuel Querido and Allert de Lange in Amsterdam, for instance, were two of a few editors who tried to support those émigré writers. Querido paid with his life for publishing the German exiles in the Netherlands. Shortly after its occupation, Querido was made prisoner. In an act of vengeance, he was killed by the Nazis in the gas chambers of Sobibor in 1943.

Curiously enough, editors not only published the ousted German novelists but also German translations of John Dos Passos, so that the exiled writers in particular could keep up with one of their key-influencers.

In 1939, Dos Passos's *The Big Money* appeared in a German translation (*Der große Schatten*) by Klaus Lambrecht in Zurich and Prague.

Lambrecht had been born in Weimar in 1912. He studied at the University of Jena, becoming a journalist and eventually a translator. His translations into German include American best-selling novels by Sinclair Lewis, John Steinbeck, and Richard Wright.

In 1936, Lambrecht and his wife Irene left Germany. He explained the reasons for their departure by stating,

> It was our own voluntary decision to leave and did neither result from racial causes, as we both are no Jews, nor had we any political reasons except that of

> our democratic conviction and the wish
> for individual and spiritual freedom.
> (Kelletat 2022: n.p.)

Lambrecht lived for some time in Paris,[13] where he made his living

> by placing books with German publishing
> houses outside Germany, chiefly in
> Switzerland [Zurich], and translating
> these books into the German language.
> (Kelletat 2022: n.p.)

As stated, John Dos Passos's *Der große Schatten* appeared in Zurich as well as in Prague. The German version of *The Big Money* was edited by the Büchergilde Gutenberg, which had a licensing agreement with Bermann Fischer and both published in these two cities.

---

[13] Later Klaus Lambrecht settled in the USA, where he worked as radio script writer.

John Dos Passos's scholar, Jessica Teague, alerted me of the existence of a letter, dated February 27, 1936, by Dos Passos's literary agents, archived at the Special Collections Library of the University of Virginia, that referred to this German edition of *The Big Money*.

At the time, the German editor Rowohlt wanted to publish Dos Passos's novel. Yet, the writer's literary agents were aware of Nazi censorship and the great difficulties that Rowohlt would have to put up with. Therefore, it was stressed in the letter that it might have been more reasonable to publish Dos Passos's *The Big Money* in Zurich. The letter reads:

> I'm afraid poor Rowohlt's affairs are going from bad to worse [...]. In any case, as Bermann Fischer is opening shortly in Zurich, where he will be able to publish Mr. Dos Passos without interference from the Nazi government, I think quite

the best plan will be to let him see THE BIG MONEY before offering it to any other German publisher. ("Publisher related correspondence with Dos Passos" n.p.)

Actually, Dos Passos's *The Big Money* only appeared three years later. But it did come out in Zurich and Prague.

John Dos Passos: republished in West Germany

With the fall of Nazism and the unconditional surrender of Germany to the Allied Powers at the end of WWII, in May 1945, John Dos Passos was sent by *Life Magazine* to report, among others, on the *Nürnberger Prozesse* (Nuremberg Trials). Erich Kästner, who also had been admitted to the Palace of Justice of the International Military Tribunal to report for the *Neue Zeitung* (*New Newspaper*), remembers having seen Dos Passos there. Standing in awe, Kästner did not dare to approach his famous American colleague, who had been authorized to visit

the penitentiary in which the Nazi leaders had been imprisoned facing the accusation of having committed crimes

141

against humanity. [Dos Passos] talked to Colonel Andrus, responsible for the prisoners, among who were Hess that paid 'no attention to anything,' and Goering, whom Dos Passos described as always feeling 'selfimportant.' Further, Dos Passos [...] commented on Sidney Alderman reading the indictment; 'All day the reading goes on. [...] Shooting, starvation and torture... tortured and killed... shooting, beating and hanging... shooting, starvation and torture.' Without comment, [Dos Passos] also reported that the 'defendants pled *nicht schuldig* [not guilty].' (Qtd. in Oliveira 2013: 395)

In 1946, Dos Passos reorganized the articles previously published in *Life Magazine* in a book format under the title: *Tour of Duty*. The monograph was only partially translated into German by Michael Kleeberg in the late 1990's as: *Das Land des Fragebogens, 1945: Reportagen aus dem besiegten Deutschland* (*The Land of the Questionnaire, 1945: Reportages from Defeated Germany).*

In fact, in the immediate post-war era, the West German people came up with an exculpatory concept that they called "*Stunde Null*" (zero hour), which metaphorically stood for starting again from scratch by repressing the past. The country's recent history, under the swastika, was faded out of the German collective consciousness. The German people, one might claim, felt ashamed of the horrors and the atrocities committed in the Jewish ghettos, the concentration camps, and on the battle fields. The burden was too heavy to be borne. They wanted to forget. All efforts were channeled into the reconstruction of their country that warfare had laid waste. They wanted to rebuild their lives rather than face their paralyzing guiltiness or discuss the existence of the *Kollektivschuld* (collective guilt). No time was lost with grief. The Germans were unable to sorrow their lost sons and daughters, mothers and fathers.

Cordelia Edvardson, who survived the concentration camps Theresienstadt and Auschwitz, criticized the German people for this attempted form of amnesia:

> "We Germans have never mourned, not even our own dead." Instead, you have invented the *Stunde Null*, for you and your descendants for comfort and relief. Our six million murdered men, women, and children—the dead of other peoples, including your own—can never be reduced to zero. [...] The *Stunde Null*, as if the German people could get out of history and start from the beginning; extinguish what has been done, just like one erases a blackboard. [...] With the *Stunde Null*, with this sponge, you also erased us, your victims, the living and the dead, wiped us out once again. (1991: 43)

Wanting to forget, Dos Passos's *Tour of Duty* was, at this time, no book that the German people could have read. The social dealing with their past and committed crimes was repressed until the late 1950's/early 1960's. Only then did the *Vergangenheitsbewältigung* (coming to terms with the past) gradually set in, i.e., the critical discussion about the National-Socialist regime, with all its historic and legal implications, like financial compensations to its victims.

In West Germany, the military authority that represented the Allied Powers did not want to force the German people to confront the darkest chapter of German history, even though sporadically film material about the Holocaust and Nazism was publicly exhibited.

Now, in the immediate post-war era, the military authority did implement a new form of censorship this time to prevent and repress the survival of Nazi ideas. In 1945/1946, all racist books were ordered to be destroyed.

Henceforth, all books allowed to be published had to be submitted to the Allies' goal of *Umerziehung*—reeducating the German population to embrace freedom and democracy.

As soon as 1946, the Allies used the *Fragebogen* (questionnaire) that all Germans had to answer straightforwardly to decide on how much each person had been infected by Nazism. A chart differed among "major culprits," those that were "guilty," "fellow travelers," and those that were above suspicion. (Balzer 1990: 432)

If the person was found guilty, he or she was inhibited from carrying out functions in any positions of influence, like in the new German administration, government, universities,[14] police forces, etc... In *Century's Ebb* Dos Passos observed:

> There were stiff jail penalties for lying on your fragebogen. If it turned out from your fragebogen that you'd been a member of the Nazi Party, you couldn't exercise any trade or profession. All you could do was pick and shovel work. (1975: 212)

Also, cultural institutions, like theaters, were cleansed of anyone suspicious of having been a resilient Nazi supporter.

During this phase of transitioning from the Nazi culture to a new, democratic German culture, the arts, music, and literature were actually imported. The

---

[14] Among the university professors who lost their position was Martin Heidegger, who was prohibited to teach and to publish (*Lehr- und Publikationsverbot*) until 1951.

Amerika Haus (America House), the British Center, the *Centre Culturel Français* (French Cultural Center), and the House of Culture of the Soviet Union represented all Allied cultures, whose aim it was "to convey the spirit of anti-fascism, humanism, and democracy" to the German people. (Glaser 1997: 101)

The latter were now apprehensively turning their noses up at all writers that had been acknowledged by the Nazis. The exiled authors were requested to come back home, even though many Germans openly criticized them for having deserted the German people. (See Balzer 1990: 434)

In the meantime, the new constitution of the *Bundesrepublik Deutschland* (Federal Republic of Germany), ratified in May 1949, established in its Article 5 that "no censorship" existed. Nevertheless, legal exemptions were possible according to the

Jugendschutzgesetz (youth protection legislation) to protect young people, once more, from "pornography and trash literature." (Wilpert 1989: 1048)

Furthermore, defamatory writings (libel and slander) were declared illicit. *Volksverhetzung* (incitement to hatred), *Hetzschriften* (inflammatory writings), such as *Mein Kampf*, that glorified and incited war, racial hatred, and crime were, also, declared unlawful.

In the nineteen-nineties, denial of the Nazi genocide, known as the *Auschwitzlüge* (Auschwitz lie) was added to the *Strafgesetzbuch* (German penal code) and has since been considered a criminal offense.

Notwithstanding, the West German publishers found it necessary to republish John Dos Passos's *Manhattan Transfer* as soon as possible. One of the country's pressing aims was, as indicated, the denazification of Germany and its democratization. The publishing house Suhrkamp had thus decided in 1948, at a time of great misery where people had not enough money to buy food, not to mention books, to run the risk and reedit Paul Baudisch's translation of *Manhattan Transfer*. It seems rather foolish to publish books at a time when

> sugar, rice, fat, chocolate, coffee, and cigarettes [were] coveted wealth, and many willingly traded their hard-saved *Meissen* porcelain for butter and canned meat. The black market and prostitution flourished because of hunger; it was easy to obtain a night of love for a pound of bread. (Qtd. in Oliveira 2008b: 106)

And yet, it was deemed important to republish John Dos Passos's novel, which was to make people think again and to educate them to finally embrace freedom, liberty, and democracy, to end racism and discrimination against Jews, according to the directives of the Allies.

In 1960, *Manhattan Transfer* came out in a second edition, this time by Rowohlt; that same year, Rowohlt also reedited successfully Julian Gumperz' translation of *Three Soldiers*.

Paul Baudisch's translation of *Manhattan Transfer* that Kurt Tucholsky described as "clean and decent" (Panter 1928: 287) was only replaced in 2016, by Dirk van Gunsteren, who produced a new translation of the famous novel for a German radio play adaptation and a new paperback edition by Rowohlt.

John Dos Passos: republished in East Germany

In the DDR, (*Deutsche Demokratische Republik*—German Democratic Republic), the *Stunde Null* did not exist. The Soviets insisted that the German people were to be confronted with their history and guilt. Journalists were ordered to write about the horrors of the concentration camps.

Nico Rost published *Goethe in Dachau* that described in great detail how Jews were systematically exterminated through starvation, hard labor, torture, and non-medical treatment. (See Balzer 1990: 461)

Yet soon, in 1948, Walter Ulbricht, the chairman of the state council, complained that writers were only dealing with the past instead of writing about the present: the fight to create a 'superior socialist system' within the East German Republic.

Even though the country's constitution of 1949 declared that the DDR practiced no censorship and that books were not to be forbidden, the truth was that manuscripts had to be allowed to be printed in the first place. It was thus an inverted form of censorship.

Editors that intended to publish a book needed to obtain a *Druckgenehmigung* (printing permit) from the *Ministerium für Kultur* (Ministry of Culture) before they could print and release the book.

A writer who wanted to see his work published had to support the socialist state order. If he was known to be an advocate of communism, he easily would obtain such a printing license. Yet, works that were criticizing or opposing the regime got no authorization, which ultimately meant the book could not be published. The regime then claimed that there was not sufficient paper to be spared on the book project.

To be true, the DDR suffered from a shortage of paper and had to impose *Papierkontingente* (paper quota) on each publisher, but this fact was too often used as an excuse to swindle about censorship.

Each text submitted for publication had to be reviewed by two censors officially referred to as 'external referees.' Herewith it was granted that nothing would be published that could annoy the SED (*Sozialistische Einheitspartei Deutschland* —German Socialist Unity Party).

Unequivocally, John Dos Passos's early work was downright leftist; in it he criticized the exploitation of industrial societies, exposing capitalist abuses. And yet, it took until the 1970's to reedit Dos Passos's works. The West German Rowohlt *Verlag* had worked out a licensing agreement with the East Aufbau *Verlag*, so that Paul Baudisch's translation of *Manhattan Transfer* could finally be published in 1974.

Five years later, Baudisch's translation of *The 42nd Parallel* appeared as well in the East with an epilogue by Günther Klotz[15] that was considered in the *Druckgenehmigung* "an important key to understand this reading-worthy book." (*Bundesarchiv* 1979: n.p.) Ironically, the *Gutachten* (report) had been written by Günther Klotz himself and Klaus Schirrmeister.[16]

---

[15] Günther Klotz was born in May 1925 in Berlin. He worked for the Aufbau *Verlag*, where he published and commented on William Shakespeare's comedies. He also translated Mark Twain into German. Klotz became a specialist in English and American studies at the *Deutsche Akademie der Wissenschaften* (German Academy of Sciences of the GDR). He died in 2001.

[16] As Klotz, Klaus Schirrmeister also worked for the Aufbau *Verlag* as a translator. He translated Charles

The German translation of *Nineteen Nineteen* was also published in 1979, while *The Big Money* (*Die Hochfinanz*) was only published in 1981, yet each of the above is listed with a first run of 10,000 copies.

The Aufbau *Verlag* had no money to order a new translation. It was cheaper to sign the contract with Rowohlt. This information was made available by Thomas Überfoff, the editorial director at Rowohlt, per e-mail correspondence, on May 24, 2016.

Überhoff further remembered that Rowohlt was regularly allowed to exhibit its books during the Leipzig book fair. Yet the books were displayed in a cordoned-off area. Only 10 people were let in at once. The others had to wait for their turn in a queue. The publisher was forbidden to sell its books, and the readers were prohibited

Dickens into German, as well as mystery stories by Amy Myers.

to take them with them. Yet, as stressed by Überhoff, Rowohlt's collaborators at the book fair often enough closed their eyes so that the people could steal the books in exhibition. Nonetheless, the thieves had to be careful not to get caught by the authorities that would search them thoroughly when leaving.

Überhoff could not remember if Dos Passos's books had been under those that were stolen. In any case, it might be speculated that the book fair opened an illicit door for a very limited number of readers to get access to Dos Passos's writings, way before they were officially approved and printed in the GDR.

In the epilogue by Günther Klotz, commended by the censors in the printing permission, the author stressed that Dos Passos was the "most important revolutionary writer." (Dos Passos 1982:

667) Klotz emphasized Dos Passos leftist concerns by stating:

> Like no other American bourgeois writer, [Dos Passos] was committed to the working class. In 1926 he participates in setting up the left-wing journal "New Masses," for which he then wrote cultural and literary articles and reported on the class struggle in the country. (Dos Passos 1982: 679)

Furthermore, Klotz highlighted Dos Passos's engagement with the running of a leftist theater (New Playwright Theater), for which Dos Passos had written, among others, the *Streikdrama* (strike play) *Airways Inc.*.

Klotz also referred to Dos Passos's defense of Sacco and Vanzetti and the writer's visit to the Soviet Union, failing however to mention Dos Passos's disillusionment with the dictatorship of the proletariat. As denoted by Vakhtang Amaglobeli, Dos Passos described critically the life in "Batumi and Tbilisi after their annexation by the 11th Red Army" in his article "The Caucasus under the Soviets"; the writer unfolded about the "mess, chaos, disappointment among the people, unemployment and poverty." (Amaglobeli 2010: 59)

> What perturbed Dos Passos had to do with how the population was treated in the communist country. [...] In a letter to his friend, the communist writer, Edmund Wilson, dated January 1935, Dos Passos [...] explained: 'My enthusiastic feelings [...] about the U.S.S.R. have been on a continual decline since the early days.' (Qtd. in Oliveira 2013: 202-203)

Instead, Klotz wrote: Dos Passos "visited the Soviet Union, whose socialism was for many Americans a real alternative to the American social system." (Dos Passos 1979: 542)

Additionally, Klotz claimed that Dos Passos's novels were a voice "against the imperialist reality" (Dos Passos 1979: 536) and that it were not the poor, which had "failed" in his novels "but the social system" itself. (Dos Passos 1982: 677)

Klotz brought up as well Dos Passos's thumbnail biography on Minor Keith, agreeing with the writer's accusations of Keith being an exploiter, whose workers had to die for his greediness. (See Dos Passos 1979: 547) In *The 42nd Parallel*, the first novel of Dos Passos's *U.S.A.* trilogy, the author writes wryly:

> while the working people "died of whisky, malaria, yellow jack, [and] dysentery [...] Minor Keith didn't die." Keith built a railroad in Limon, Jamaica; his workers came all from New Orleans. Seven hundred workers were earning a

mere "dollar a day. [...] Of that bunch about twentyfive came out alive. The rest left their whiskyscalded carcasses to rot in the swamps. [...] Minor Keith was only interested in his profits; it did not affect him that his workers died. He used them up to exhaustion and gave them whisky so they would not dispute for higher wages. Keith became a wealthy man, but to Dos Passos he was [indeed, as righteously interpreted by Günther Klotz,] an atrocious character, a man of no scruples. (Oliveira 2013: 275)

Nonetheless, Klotz did not hide that Dos Passos, later on in his life, distanced himself from socialism and that he became conservative. Klotz observed somewhat contemptuously that after that, John Dos Passos had "produced nothing new or of any importance." (Dos Passos 1982: 685) This remark is, of course, wrong and is owed to the fact that the political conviction of the Dos Passos in his later life clashed with that of Günther Klotz. In this context, I express my agreement with Lowell Fredric Lynde, who wrote:

> Too often, using their own political positions as guidelines, the books of Dos Passos have been judged on how well they conformed to the political opinions of the reviewers. This has held true for the critics on both the left and the right. What they have exercised is a kind of literary political censorship. (1967: 246)

Quod erat demonstrandum

In this monograph, I outlined the reasons why John Dos Passos's books were first burned and then banned during National-Socialism in Germany. The fact that Dos Passos's works were considered modern, immoral, anarcho-communist, or anti-militarist led the Nazis to fear his literary prowess and the influence he exercised over his readership as a free thinking, high-quality, independent writer. His openness, his sharp disapproval of racism, bigotry, and anti-Semitism, and his objection against Nazism were reason enough for the Nazis to outlaw and dread Dos Passos's entire work of contemporary chronicles that mirrored and represented society as it (mal-)functioned, and with which he could have inspired his readers to resent and amend political and economic standards.

I have also shown what happened to other authors in Germany during the same period of time, focusing, of course, on Dos Passos's translators Paul Baudisch, Julian Gumperz, and Klaus Lambrecht who were compelled to flee to foreign countries.

In addition, I stressed what the new literature, approved by the Nazis, was about and how it was perceived by the majority of the German readers up to that time.

I also disclosed the reasons why John Dos Passos could not have conformed to the new nature of literature that was being conceived in Nazi Germany.

Furthermore, I covered the post-war era in which John Dos Passos's *oeuvre* was reprinted in both West and East Germany. In this context, I mentioned and commented on the relevance of printing permits in the German Democratic Republic and the way they applied to blue-penciling.

Finally, it is important to emphasize that John Dos Passos never approved of any form of censorship throughout his life. As a writer, he always demanded freedom of expression, and as a citizen of the world, he urged recognition of his and others' fundamental rights to self-determination.

He could not have chosen a better title for a collection of articles and essays he reprinted in 1956, and with which he summarized his lifetime literary leitmotif, *The Theme is Freedom*.

A short biographical note
on John Dos Passos

John Roderigo Dos Passos was born in Chicago, January 14, 1896; he died on September 28, 1970. He was a *Luso-*American writer and painter, whose work was critical as well as socially and politically engaging.

Manoel Joaquim dos Passos, the writer's paternal grandfather, was born in Ponta do Sol, Madeira.

In 1830, at the age of eighteen, he decided to emigrate to the United States to escape military service. (Cf. Oliveira 2013: 82) He settled in Philadelphia as a shoemaker and married Lucinda Ann Cattell, with whom he had nine children.

The fourth child, John Randolph Dos Passos, was born on July 31, 1844.

He began working at an early age to support his family. He studied law and was admitted to the Pennsylvania Bar in 1865.

Two years later he moved to New York, where he made a name for himself as a criminal defense lawyer.

In 1882, John Randolph Dos Passos published a treatise on the law of stockbrokers and stock-exchanges, which became compulsory reading for law students.

The prestigious lawyer began to represent publically traded companies, and became the highest-paid lawyer on Wall Street.

John Randolph married Mary Dyckman Hays. Sometime later, he met Lucy Addison Sprigg Madison, with whom he had an extramarital relationship.

On January 14, 1896, his son John Roderigo Madison was born in a hotel in Chicago. To avoid any scandal, his mistress

Lucy Madison and their son emigrated to Europe, living in various hotels in Belgium.

In 1906, Lucy and John Madison returned to the United States, where John was enrolled at the Choate School.

On March 20, 1910, Mary Hays died, and John Randolph Dos Passos married Lucy Madison on June 21. From now on, John Madison took on his father's surname, signing his future literary works with John Dos Passos.

In 1912, the young man was admitted to Harvard University, where he graduated with honors in European Languages and Literature.

In 1917, he enlisted in the Norton-Harjes Ambulance Unit to take part in the First World War as an ambulance driver, serving during the battle of Verdun. After the signing of the armistice, John Dos Passos was allowed to stay in France to study anthropology at the Sorbonne

University. As a result of his experience as an ambulance driver during the First World War, John Dos Passos published *Three Soldiers* in 1921, his first international success.

In the same year, John Dos Passos traveled to Portugal[17] accompanied by his friend, the poet e. e. cummings. Both visited the Azores (Fayal), Madeira, Lisbon, Coimbra, and Oporto. On this trip, John Dos Passos read *Os Lusíadas* (*The Lusiads*) by Luís Vaz de Camões in Portuguese. Aware of his Portuguese ancestry, the writer tried several times to learn Portuguese and to read the works of Portuguese literary classics such as Antero

---

[17] Dos Passos travelled extensively throughout his life; he visited, among others, Egypt, Greece, Italy, Turkey, Spain, France, Armenia, Azerbaijan, Iraq, Georgia, Iran, the desert of Damascus, Morocco, Mexico, the U.S.S.R., Jamaica, Cuba, Ecuador, Japan, Germany, Austria, Brazil, Switzerland, Peru, Chile (Easter Island), and Canada.

de Quental, Fernando Pessoa, and Eça de Queirós.

In 1925, John Dos Passos published *Manhattan Transfer*, which is considered to be one of his masterpieces and, since 1999, has been included in *Le Monde*'s famous list of the 100 best books of the 20th century.

On August 19, 1929, John Dos Passos married Katharine Smith.

In the mid-1930s, John Dos Passos became the first writer to make the cover of *Time Magazine*.

In 1937, John Dos Passos went to Spain as a correspondent to witness the Civil War up close, severely criticizing the *coup d'état* led by General Francisco Franco.

A year later, three of his novels, *The 42nd Parallel* (1930), *Nineteen Nineteen* (1932), and *The Big Money* (1936) were brought together in a trilogy published under the title: *U.S.A.*. The French philosopher Jean-Paul Sartre, who was deeply inspired by the work, considered John Dos Passos "the greatest writer of [his] time." (Qtd. in Oliveira 2013: 25)

During the Third Reich, Dos Passos's books were first burned (in 1933) and later (in 1938) banned by the Nazis.

In 1945, John Dos Passos was sent as a war correspondent to Germany, Austria, and the Pacific. In this role, he covered the Nuremberg trials for *Life Magazine* and commented on the social and political problems of the immediate post-war period.

In September 1947, John Dos Passos was involved in a car accident. His wife, Katharine, died at the scene while the writer was seriously injured, losing the sight in his right eye.

On August 6, 1949, John Dos Passos married Elizabeth Holdridge.

On May 15, 1950, their daughter Lucy Hamlin Dos Passos was born.

At the end of the 1960s, John Dos Passos once again traveled to Portugal to do research at the *Torre do Tombo* Archive for a book on the history of his ancestors' country, which he published in 1969 under the title, *The Portugal Story: Three Centuries of Exploration and Discoveries*.

In the 1950s, John Dos Passos received several distinctions. In addition to the honorary doctorate awarded to him by the Northwestern University, the writer was honored by his *alma mater* by being inducted as an honorary member of the famous Phi Beta Kappa academic society at Harvard University.

In 1957, John Dos Passos received America's highest literary award: the Gold Medal of the National Institute of Arts and Letters, presented to him by Nobel laureate William Faulkner.

In the 1960s, John Dos Passos also won the Peter Francisco Award from the Portuguese Continental Union and the Antonio Feltrinelli Prize from the *Accademia Nazionale dei Lincei* in Italy. In addition, the writer was invited as writer-in-residence by the University of Virginia, to which he donated his papers, including some of his works of art (during his lifetime he created over 400 paintings), his manuscripts, diaries, and correspondence.

The writer's work was also recognized in Madeira. In 1960, during a trip to the island with his wife, Elizabeth, and his daughter Lucy, the mayor of Ponta do Sol, Joaquim Sequeira Cabrita, paid tribute to John Dos Passos by placing a commemorative plaque next to Villa Passos, a building that belonged to the writer's ancestors and which was converted into the John Dos Passos Cultural Center in 2004.

The same year, Dos Passos was also honored in Kutaisi, Georgia, with a commemorative plaque, placed at the building (formerly known as the Hotel de France) where the writer stayed for two nights in the nineteen-twenties.

John Dos Passos died of a heart attack on September 28, 1970, in Baltimore and was buried in Westmoreland, Virginia.

Throughout his life John Dos Passos published: *One Man's Initiation* (1920), *Three Soldiers* (1921), *Rosinante to the Road Again* (1922), *A Pushcart at the Curb* (1922), *Streets of Night* (1923), *Manhattan Transfer* (1925), *Orient Express* (1927), *Facing the Chair* (1927), *The 42nd Parallel* (1930), *Nineteen Nineteen* (1932), *In All Countries* (1934), *Three Plays* (1934), *The Big Money* (1936), *The Villages Are the Heart of Spain* (1937), *U.S.A.* (1938), *Journeys between Wars* (1938), *Adventures of a Young Man* (1939), *The Living*

Thoughts of Tom Paine (1940), *The Ground We Stand On* (1941), *Number One* (1943), *State of the Nation* (1944), *First Encounter* (1945), *Tour of Duty* (1946), *The Grand Design* (1949), *The Prospect before Us* (1950), *Chosen Country* (1951), *District of Columbia* (1952), *The Head and Heart of Thomas Jefferson* (1954), *Most Likely to Succeed* (1954), *The Theme Is Freedom* (1956), *The Men Who Made the Nation* (1957), *The Great Days* (1958), *Prospects of a Golden Age* (1959), *Midcentury* (1961), *Mr. Wilson's War* (1962), *Brazil on the Move* (1963), *Occasions and Protests* (1964), *Thomas Jefferson: the Making of a President* (1964), *The Shackles of Power* (1966), *The World in a Glass* (1966), *The Best Times* (1966), *The Portugal Story* (1969). Posthumously appeared *Easter Island, Island of Enigmas* (1971); *The Fourteenth Chronicle: Letters and Diaries by John Dos Passos* (1973) edited by

Charles Townsend Ludington; *Century's Ebb* (1975); as well as *Afterglow and Other Undergraduate Writings* (1990), the latter published by Richard Layman.

Bibliography

ALLEN, Alice Jacob. (1966). *World War I in the Novels of John Dos Passos*. [M.A.] Texas: Rice University.

AMAGLOBELI, Vakthang. "John Dos Passos on the Annexation of Georgia in 1921". In Maria Zina Abreu. *John Dos Passos, Biography and Critical Essays*. Newcastle upon Tyne: Cambridge Scholars Publishing (2010): 56-62.

"Australian Book Censorship". *The Argus*. (Friday 3 May, 1935): 10.

BALZER, Bernd. (1990). *Deutsche Literatur in Schaglichtern*. Mannheim: Meyers Lexikon Verlag.

BAUTISTA, Rosa. (2016). *A Descriptive Analysis of the Spanish Translations of Manhattan Transfer and their Role in the Spanish Construction of John Dos Passos*. [Ph.D.] Madrid: Universidad Autónoma de Madrid.

BECKER, Konrad. et al. (2002). *Die Politik der Infosphäre, WorldInformation.Org.* Bonn: Bundeszentrale für politische Bildung.

BLANCHFIELD, Patrick. "The Last Days of Sigmund Freud". In *The New Republic.* (1 September 2022): n.p.

BONSAVER, Guido. (2007). *Censorship and Literature in Fascist Italy.* Toronto: University of Toronto Press.

BOYER, Paul. (2002). *Purity in Print, Book Censorship in America from the Gilded Age to the Computer Age.* Madison: University of Wisconsin Press.

Bundesarchiv. (1979). "John Dos Passos: *Der 42. Breitengrad*, Gutachten: Günther Klotz, Klaus Schirrmeister". [L – P; Druck-Nr. 120/170/79; Aufbau Verlag Berlin und Weimar].

BRUNNER, Detlev. (2013). *Verbrannt, geraubt, gerettet Bücherverbrennungen in Deutschland, Eine Ausstellung der*

Bibliothek der Friedrich-Ebert-Stiftung anlässlich des 70. Jahrestages. Vol. 13. Bonn: Bibliothek der Friedrich-Ebert-Stiftung.

COONEY, John. (2000). *John Charles McQuaid: Ruler of Catholic Ireland*. New York: Syracuse University Press.

DOS PASSOS, John. (1975). *Century's Ebb: The Thirteenth Chronicle*. Boston: Gambit.

----------. (1979). *Der 42. Breitengrad*. Berlin: Aufbau Verlag.

----------. (1982). *Die Hochfinanz*. Berlin: Aufbau Verlag.

----------. (1967). *District of Columbia*. [The trilogy contains: *Adventures of a Young Man*, *Number One*, and the *Grand Design*] Boston: Houghton Mifflin.

----------. (1986). *Manhattan Transfer*. London: Penguin.

----------. "Thank You, Mr. Hitler". In *Common Sense* I. (27 April 1933): 13.

----------. (1956). *The Theme Is Freedom*. New York: Dodd, Mead and Co..

----------. (2003). *Travel Books and Other Writings 1916-1941*. Charles Townsend Ludington. (ed.). New York: The Library of America.

EDVARDSON, Cordelia. (1991). *Die Welt zusammenfügen*. München: dtv.

EHM, Rainer. "Der 12. Mai 1933: Als in Regensburg die Bücher brannten". In Monika Franz. *Einsichten und Perspektiven*, München: Bayerische Landeszentrale für politische Bildungsarbeit, No. 1 (2013): 4-19.

ENDERLE, Luiselotte. (1999). *Erich Kästner*. Hamburg: Rowohlt.

GIROD, Sonja. (2012). *Protest und Revolte—Drei Jahrhunderte studentisches Aufbegehren in der Universitätsstadt Göttingen (1737 bis 2000)*. [Ph.D.] Göttingen: Georg-August-Universität Göttingen.

GLASER, Hermann. (1997). *Deutsche Kultur, ein historischer Überblick von 1945 bis zur Gegenwart.* Bonn: Bundeszentrale für politische Bildung.

GREEN, Jonathon. (2005). *Encyclopedia of Censorship.* New York: Facts on File.

GUSSEK, Anja. (2009). *Öffentliche Zensur und Bücherverbrennung in Münster, Eine Dokumentation herausgegeben aus Anlass der Enthüllung einer Gedenktafel am 6. Mai 2009.* Münster: Eigenverlag.

HAARER, Johanna. (1939). *Mutter, erzähl von Adolf Hitler, Ein Buch zum Vorlesen, Nacherzählen und Selbstlesen für kleinere und größere Kinder.* München: J. F. Lehmanns Verlag.

HEIDEGGER, Martin. "*Nur noch ein Gott kann uns retten*: *Spiegel*-Gespräch *mit Martin Heidegger am* 23. Sept. 1966". In *Der Spiegel,* No. 23 (May 1976): 193-219.

----------. (2000). *Reden und andere Zeugnisse eines Lebensweges* (1910–

1976), Gesamtausgabe, Band 16. Frankfurt am Main: Vittorio Klostermann.

HEINE, Heinrich. (2006). *Deutschland ein Wintermärchen, Geschrieben im Januar 1844.* Berlin: Berliner Wissenschafts-verlag.

HERTBRUGGEN, Anneleen von. (2019). *Des Deutschen Dichters Sendung, Die Sakralisierung von "Führer", "Reich" und "Volk" in der nationalsozialistischen Dichtung: Heinrich Anacker, Gerhard Schumann und Herybert Menzel.* [Ph.D.] Antwerpen: Universiteit Antwerpen.

HORVÁTH, Ödön von. (2012). *Youth without God.* New York: Melville House.

IANNACCARO, Giuliana. (2014). *Enforcing and Eluding Censorship: British and Anglo-Italian Perspectives.* New Castle upon Tyne: Cambridge Scholars Publishing.

JONES, Derek. (2015). *Censorship, A World Encyclopedia*. Vol. 1 – 4, New York: Routledge.

JÜNGER, Ernst. (1996). *The Storm of Steel, From the Diary of a German Strom-Troop Officer on the Western Front*. New York: Howard Fertig.

KÄSTNER, Erich. (1997). *Bei Durchsicht meiner Bücher*. München: dtv.

KELLETAT, Andreas. (2022). "Klaus Lambrecht, 1912 - ?". In Germersheimer Übersetzer-Lexikon UeLEX (online). – accessed on November 7, 2024.

KRISCHKE, Traugott. (1998a). *Horváths Jugend ohne Gott*. Frankfurt am Main: Suhrkamp.

----------. (1998b). *Ödön von Horváth, Kind seiner Zeit*. Berlin: Ullstein.

LAMPRECHT, Niko. (2015) *Musik im Nationalsozialismus. Ideologie, Propaganda, Widersprüche. (Geschichts-*

unterricht praktisch). Schwalbach am Tanaus Wochenschau Verlag 2015.

LEWY, Guenter. (2016). *Harmful and Undesirable, Book Censorship in Nazi Germany*. New York: Oxford University Press.

LOCKHARDT, William. "Literature, the Law of Obscenity, and the Constitution". In *Minnesota Law Review*, Vol. 38, No. 4 (March 1954): 295-395.

LOHMANN, Hans-Martin. (2002). *Sigmund Freud*. Hamburg: Rowohlt.

LOOBY, Robert. (2015). *Censorship, Translation and English Language Fiction in People's Poland*. Leiden: Brill Rodopi.

LUDINGTON, Charles Townsend. (2016). "E-Mail correspondence, 11 February".

----------. (1980). *John Dos Passos, A Twentieth-Century Odyssey*. New York: Dutton.

LYNDE, Lowell Fredric. (1967). *John Dos Passos, The Theme is Freedom.* [Ph.D.] Louisiana: Louisiana State University.

NANNEY, Lisa. (1998). *John Dos Passos Revisited.* New York: Twayne Publishers.

NAWROCKA, Irene. (2000). *Verlagssitz: Wien, Stockholm, New York, Amsterdam. Der Bermann-Fischer Verlag im Exil, 1933-1950, Ein Abschnitt aus der Geschichte des S. Fischer Verlages.* Frankfurt am Main: Archiv für Geschichte des Buchwesens.

NESKE, Gunther. (1990). *Martin Heidegger and National Socialism.* New York: Paragon House.

NICOLAI, Andreas. (2010). *Bäuerliches Erbrecht in rechtshistorischer und vergleichender Sicht.* Graz: Universität Graz.

OLIVEIRA, Miguel. (2008a). *Classified and Confidential, F.B.I. File N.º 97-2497,*

Subject: John Dos Passos. Norderstedt: BoD.

----------. (2013). *From a Man without a Country to an American by Choice: John Dos Passos and Migration*. Norderstedt: BoD.

----------. (2008b). *John Dos Passos' Influence on Günter Grass, A Study on Two Memory-Writers and Two Distinct Approaches towards Migration as a Literary Theme.* Norderstedt: BoD.

----------. "Military Migration in John Dos Passos's *Three Soldiers*". In Maria Zina Abreu. *John Dos Passos, Biography and Critical Essays*. Newcastle upon Tyne: Cambridge Scholars Publishing (2010): 199-207.

PANTER, Peter. "Auf dem Nachttisch". In *Die Weltbühne*, Vol. 24, (1928): 287.

PETERSEN, Klaus. (1995). *Zensur in der Weimarer Republik*. Stuttgart: Metzler Verlag.

"Publisher related correspondence with Dos Passos". (27 February 1936) [Special Collections Library of the University of Virginia, "Dos Passos File", Box 18-20, Brandt and Brandt 1929-1957, Folder – (3 of 11)].

"Relatório de Censura". No. 6943, (1961). ["*Aventures d'un Jeune Homme*". Torre do Tombo, Lisbon.]

ROMMEL, Kathleen. (2012). *"We only have words against/ Power Superpower": Literary Politics and the Subversion of Imperialism in Dos Passos's U.S.A.*. [M.A.] North Carolina: Wake Forest University.

SCHLOSSER, Horst Dieter. (1994). *dtv-Atlas zur deutschen Literatur, Tafeln und Texte*. München: dtv.

SCHMIDT, Uwe. (2008). *National-sozialistische Schulverwaltung in Hamburg, Vier Führungspersonen*. Hamburg: Hamburg University Press.

SCHNEIDER, Ulrich. (2013). *Wo man Bücher verbrennt, verbrennt man am Ende auch Menschen, Zur Erinnerung an die Bücherverbrennungen am 10. Mai 1933*. Frankfurt am Main: Vereinigung der Verfolgten des Naziregimes.

SCHRÖTER, Klaus. (2002). *Heinrich Mann*. Hamburg: Rowohlt.

----------. (1998). *Thomas Mann*. Hamburg: Rowohlt.

Verzeichnis englischer und nordamerikanischer Schriftsteller, Reichsministerium für Volksaufklärung und Propaganda, Abteilung Schrifttum. (1938). zu Leipzig: Verlag des Börsenvereins Deutscher Buchhändler.

SHERRY, Samantha. (2015). *Discourses of Regulation and Resistance: Censoring Translation in the Stalin and Khrushchev Era Soviet Union*. Edinburgh: Edinburgh University Press.

STRÄTZ, Hans-Wolfgang. "Die Studentische Aktion Wider den Undeutschen Geist im Frühjahr 1933". *Institut für Zeitgeschichte München*, No. 4, (1968): 347-372.

TURNER, Henry Ashby. (1980). *Faschismus und Kapitalismus, Studien zum Verhältnis zwischen Nationalismus und Wirtschaft.* Göttingen: Vandenhoeck und Ruprecht.

ÜBERFOFF, Thomas. (2016). "E-mail correspondence, 24 May".

WAGENER, Hans. (1996). *Lion Feuchtwanger, Köpfe des 20. Jahrhunderts.* Berlin: Morgenbuch Verlag.

WILLIG, Charles Loyed. (1964). *John Dos Passos: Art and Ideology.* [M.A.] Stillwater: Oklahoma State University.

WILPERT, Gero von. (1989). *Sachwörterbuch der Literatur.* Stuttgart: Kröner Verlag.